With Different Eyes

With Different Eyes

Insights into Teaching Language Minority Students Across the Disciplines

Edited by:

Faye Peitzman

George Gadda

University of California Los Angeles
Writing Program

Longman

With Different Eyes
Copyright © 1994 by The Regents of the University of California.
All rights reserved.
No part of this publication may be reproduced,
stored in a retrieval system, or transmitted
in any form or by any means, electronic, mechanical,
photocopying, recording, or otherwise,
without the prior permission of the publisher.

Longman Publishing Group
10 Bank Street, White Plains, New York, 10606

Editorial Director: Joanne Dresner
Acquisitions Editor: Allen Ascher
Production-Editorial & Design Director: Helen B. Ambrosio
Text Design: Woodshed Productions
Cover Design: Joseph DePinho
Production Supervisor: Richard Bretan

Library of Congress Cataloging in Publication Data
With different eyes : insights into teaching language minority
  students across the disciplines / editors, Faye Peitzman, George
  Gadda.
        p.   cm.
  Includes bibliographical references.
  ISBN 0-8013-1282-5
  1. English language—Study and teaching—Foreign speakers.
2. English language—Study and teaching—United States.
3. Interdisciplinary approach in education.   4. Language and
education—United States.   I. Peitzman, Faye.   II. Gadda, George.
PE1128.A2W575   1994
428'.007—dc20   93-33727
                                                         CIP

1 2 3 4 5 6 7 8 9 10-VG-97969594

To the Futures of Our Newest Students

AUTHORS

Donna Brinton   UCLA TESL/Applied Linguistics
Lecturer and Academic Coordinator of
ESL Service Courses

Dan Fichtner   Peninsula High School
Palos Verdes Peninsula Unified School District
ESL Literature and Science Teacher

George Gadda   UCLA Writing Programs
Coordinator of Testing

Janet Goodwin   UCLA TESL/Applied Linguistics
Lecturer

Sandra Mano   UCLA Writing Programs
Lecturer

Faye Peitzman   UCLA Center for Academic Interinstitutional
Programs
Research and Evaluation, Director of Writing
Programs

Laura Ranks   Beverly Hills High School
ESL Teacher and Coordinator

Linda Sasser   Alhambra School District
Office of Bilingual Bicultural Education
ESL Program Specialist

Beth Winningham   Monroe High School
Los Angeles Unified School District
ESL Teacher

CONTENTS

PREFACE

Our nation's educational system today faces an unprecedented challenge. At a time when the world's economy has come to demand ever more educated workers, the United States has become a center for immigration from all over the globe. Students in the Los Angeles Unified School District speak at least 90 first languages, in the Chicago city schools: 88, and in New York City: 114. Many of them expect to go on to higher education and then to professional jobs. And, indeed, our nation will need them to do so, as the information-intensive part of our economy grows and as language minority students become a larger and larger segment of our young population.

These circumstances differ profoundly from the ones the educational system confronted when waves of immigrants came to the United States from southern and eastern Europe in the latter part of the nineteenth century and the first part of the twentieth. Most of these immigrants were not highly educated; they came to the United States to take jobs in mills, mines, and factories—jobs requiring strength and diligence, but only minimal education. Typically their children finished high school and found a more secure place in the American economic system, perhaps in white-collar jobs. The third generation might go to college; by that time English was securely the family's language: the language of the school was the language of the home.

The situation of today's immigrants is much different. Partly as a result of new immigration laws giving preference to those with skills and knowledge beneficial to the United States, many of today's immigrants are highly educated business people and professionals; they expect their children to take similar roles in their new society. Parents from less privileged backgrounds have the same aspirations for their children. The schools they enter in the United States embrace cultural diversity as a value more than schools did in the early years of this century, which saw "Americanization" as a major part of their mission. And the society today's immigrants enter will have fewer and fewer opportunities for those without advanced literacy and problem-solving skills.

Thus our schools are faced with the challenge of providing an increasingly intellectual curriculum to many students who, as relative newcomers to the United States, have limited proficiency in English. Since new immigrants enter the school system at every grade level, it can't be assumed that all the instruction in the English language will be done in elementary schools. High schools in particular need to find ways to make their curriculum available to students who are bright and interested but whose English is not yet ready for classrooms designed for native speakers of English.

We call this book *With Different Eyes* because this new situation requires that we as teachers rethink some of our accustomed expectations and practices. Rather than assuming that our students are ready to learn from us primarily through the medium of the spoken word, we need to become aware of how to support the spoken word with information provided through other senses as well. Rather than assuming that command of written English should precede writing assignments, we need to incorporate writing into content courses both as a way of increasing comprehension of the course material and as a means of supporting acquisition of English. Rather than assuming that all our students understand writing tasks in the way we do, we may need to model our expectations and clarify for students how their understandings may differ from ours. Finally, we need to encourage promising limited English proficient students to make the most of their intellectual potential; in doing so, we must always be careful not to take their current levels of proficiency in English as indices of native intelligence or cognitive development.

HOW THIS BOOK CAME TO BE

This book grows out of work supported by the California Academic Partnership Program (CAPP) from 1985 to 1992. For the first three years, the UCLA Center for Academic Interinstitutional Programs (CAIP), UCLA Writing Programs, CSU Northridge, and the Los Angeles Unified School District joined in a program to give a university-level writing exam to eleventh-grade students, to help their teachers frame writing assignments leading to university-level proficiency, and to respond productively to student writing. The last two years of this effort included pilot projects involving ESL students and attempted to find how to adapt the mainstream program to their needs. Under the title "Teaching Analytical Reading and Writing," this program is still offered yearly, now by the UCLA CAIP and UCLA Writing Programs. (Throughout this book we use the terms "language minority" and "limited English proficient" [LEP] inter-changeably to refer to students in the process of acquiring English as their second language.)

In 1987–1988, CAPP funded the writing of a book based on the experience of the 1985–1987 project; the book appeared in 1988 under the title *Teaching Analytical Writing*. Once that book was finished, we proposed to CAPP a further project to adapt for ESL teachers its approaches and materials. We named an advisory committee of ESL specialists from throughout California, culled their ideas about what kinds of publications were needed in the field, and discussed their ideas with teachers we knew. As contributors to the new book we chose the authors of the chapter on limited English proficient students in *Teaching Analytical Writing* and other teachers who had made outstanding contributions to "Teaching Analytical Reading and Writing" programs. And so we set to work.

Over the next three years the authors interviewed teachers and students, visited classrooms, collected materials, and read research. As they drafted and redrafted, the emphasis of the book gradually changed. Both our advisory group and teachers in the trenches indicated a need for a practical guide to teaching sheltered content classes—classes in which teachers draw on expanded teaching methodologies to make their course content accessible to students not yet proficient in English. *With Different Eyes* now includes considerable treatment of these emerging methodologies. Though it still devotes attention to ways of assigning and responding to writing, the disciplinary focus is much broader than originally planned. We are pleased that the classroom vignettes and the writing and response samples presented in Chapters 2, 4, 5, and 6 truly come from across the curriculum. Rather than being a book just for ESL teachers, *With Different Eyes* is, as its subtitle suggests, a book for teachers of language minority students in all subject areas.

With Different Eyes was first published in California in May of 1991. Since then the book has proved very popular with teachers introduced to it through the summer institutes of California's Writing, Literature, Foreign Language, Science, and Mathematics projects, has been widely recommended by the State Department of Education's Office of Bilingual/Bicultural Education, and has been the centerpiece of a series of conferences on teaching language minority students. We are happy that the book will now reach a national audience. We believe it can provide a useful addition to preservice courses for teachers in many subjects, as well as an approachable introduction to the issues involved in teaching language minority students for teachers already working with this new population.

WHAT THIS BOOK PROVIDES

With Different Eyes offers a guide to help teachers of language minority students across the disciplines rethink their practice as teachers. Nothing suggested here is a prescription, a panacea, a final answer; final answers, we believe, would conflict with the flexible analytical perspective we hold as a value for students and teachers alike. Instead, the book raises issues and offers information— student histories, précis of ethnographic research, classroom vignettes—from which individual teachers can select or form the insights that will make them more effective teachers of LEP students. We suspect that what teachers take from these chapters may help them become more effective and reflective teachers of other students as well.

With Different Eyes has six chapters. They address in turn:

- How language minority students from diverse backgrounds have gone on to successful undergraduate careers at UCLA, and how to help more LEP students follow in their footsteps

- How teachers across the disciplines have found ways to deliver sophisticated college prep content to LEP students in sheltered classrooms
- How cultures differ in the ways they write and socialize children to use language, and how teachers can help all students to understand and succeed in the classroom
- How teachers can structure activities to help LEP students engage with the issues in difficult texts, work through the language of the texts themselves, and write analytically about what they learn
- How teachers in classes across the curriculum can assign writing to LEP students and respond to it, thus increasing both understanding of the subject matter and command of English
- How sheltered content teachers can assess their LEP students' mastery of subject matter by minimizing the language-processing demands of traditional assessment methods

In all, the book offers a perspective on how to help our schools' diverse student body succeed in the demanding academic curriculum that leads to success in higher education and in life beyond.

ACKNOWLEDGMENTS

We would first like to acknowledge the California Academic Partnership Program for funding the university–schools collaboration that produced this book. From the inception of this project Deborah Hancock, past Director of CAPP, encouraged us with her insights and enthusiasm, and current Director Frank Young has continued the CAPP tradition of energetic support.

We would also like to recognize for their contributions our two institutional partners—the Los Angeles Unified School District and UCLA—and the particular people who offered their support: Dan Isaacs, Assistant Superintendent, Senior High Division, LAUSD; Patrick Ford, past Director, UCLA Writing Programs; and Patricia Taylor, past Director of the Center for Academic Interinstitutional Programs (CAIP) in the Graduate School of Education, UCLA.

We are grateful to the many teachers who welcomed us into their sheltered classrooms: Ron Arreola, Teryne Dorret, Sandra Okura, Grant High School; Henry Chau, Alhambra High School; Tom Faigin, Monroe High School; Ron Rohac, El Cahon High School; Marie Takagaki, Artesia High School; Janeane Vigliotti, Mark Keppel High School. We also would like to acknowledge Don Campbell, University of the Pacific; Barbara Sitzman, Chatsworth High School; Todd Ullah, Jefferson High School; Barbara Wells, Culver City High School and UCLA; and Ruben Zepeda, Grant High School, for discussing and sharing the kinds of writing assignments that have been successful in their classrooms.

Thanks also to the students at UCLA and in high schools in the Alhambra, Beverly Hills, and Los Angeles Unified school districts who participated willingly in interviews, conversations, and surveys. Their honesty and insights have truly enhanced every chapter of this text.

A very special thank you to the members of our Steering Committee, who guided this project from its beginning and who read and responded to early drafts with great care: Marianne Celce-Murcia, UCLA; Barbara Kroll, CSU Northridge; June McKay, UC Berkeley; Denise Murray, CSU San José; and Tippy Schwabe, UC Davis. Thanks also to additional readers Leslie Adams, El Monte High School; Alice Addison, California State Department of Education; Don Rothman, UC Santa Cruz; Stephen Sloan, Los Angeles Unified School District; Ann Snow, CSU Los Angeles; and Patricia Taylor, UCLA, for their comments on the manuscript. In addition, conversations with Kris Gutierrez in UCLA's Graduate School of Education helped George Gadda address the issues raised in Chapter 3. Of course, any errors of fact, interpretation, or emphasis remain our own.

With Different Eyes

"YOU HAVE A CHANCE ALSO": CASE HISTORIES OF ESL STUDENTS AT THE UNIVERSITY

Donna Brinton ■ *Sandra Mano*

> You have a chance also. You have your own abilities. You can do it. You've just got to get the skills.

Speaking to language minority students still in high school, Ingrid, an emigrant student from El Salvador who is currently a sophomore at UCLA, urges her peers to pursue their goal of a higher education. Her encouraging words echo the sentiments of the thousands of immigrant students who are realizing their ambitions of attending a four-year university. They have convinced themselves that they have a chance at achieving their dream, they have the abilities that will enable them to succeed, and they have manifested the drive to achieve this dream. They have faith in their ability despite what they often see as lack of support from their family, their peers, and their teachers and counselors.

Students like these who have achieved their goal of entering higher education are of interest to all of us. They have overcome language barriers and the stress of adjusting to a new culture. For this chapter, we have interviewed nine students whom we have chosen to represent the range of backgrounds and attitudes that we as teachers have encountered in a much wider sampling of students. We interviewed these particular students because our personal contact with them created an atmosphere of mutual trust that allowed them to be candid in their remarks. Thus, this is by no means a scientific sampling of all language minority students at UCLA; we draw no conclusions about the representativeness of any of the traits described here. Our purpose is to open a window into the world of students who have beaten the odds and to illustrate their diversity. We believe these academic case histories can inform us about the processes of language learning and help us apply that knowledge in the classroom. We hope that sharing these students' histories will help us all to better understand language minority students and lead us to encourage and guide them into higher education.

THE STUDENTS' HISTORIES

The nine students we interviewed come from a variety of backgrounds and socioeconomic circumstances. Their countries of origin reflect the ethnic diversity of UCLA's undergraduate population: the students are Mexican, Salvadoran,

Taiwanese, Cambodian, Korean, Puerto Rican, and Vietnamese. They represent many other kinds of diversity as well. They range from the privileged children of upper-class families to the children of economic and political refugees; from the son of two college professors to the daughter of an undocumented welfare recipient; from a student who entered the United States at age five to one who was eighteen on entry; from students who had English instruction prior to entering the United States to students who didn't speak a word of English on entry; from students who voluntarily seek out English-speaking friends to those who avoid any contact with native English speakers; from students who come from single-family homes to those who live in an extended family situation; and finally from students who are remarkably skilled in English to those who, despite years of residence in the United States, still exhibit distinct nonnative markers in their speech and writing. In spite of their individual differences, all of these students are successfully completing their educations at UCLA. Here are their histories.

Martha: At the age of five, Martha came to the United States from Mexico with her mother and younger brother. She tells the harrowing story of having crossed the Mexican border "*El Norte* style"—across the mountains with a group of other undocumented immigrants. Without the father, who had abandoned the family, the three settled in Hollywood. The mother was assisted in obtaining work as a housekeeper by a sister who had already settled in Los Angeles. Martha recounts a childhood in which she assumed much responsibility for the family, caring for her younger brother and a younger cousin while her mother worked to support the family. Gradually, Martha also assumed responsibility for assisting her extended family with their English-language-related needs.

Martha's primary schooling was difficult, as she was one of the few Latinas in her school, and no provisions were made for her limited English proficient status. Instead, she recalls that she was passed on from grade to grade largely due to her age, with teachers ignoring her needs and classmates either ignoring or ostracizing her. It was not until fifth grade that she recalls becoming at all proficient in English; she credits her improvement to a bilingual Latino teacher who served as her mentor, encouraging her to speak English and to pursue the goal of higher education.

In seventh grade, Martha suffered a setback: she was identified for the first time as an ESL student and was required to enroll in ESL classes—an incident that took her by surprise. This incident carried with it additional consequences, since in her school district ESL students were automatically tracked into remedial classes in content areas. With some effort on Martha's part, and much discussion with her school counselors, she was able by ninth grade to enroll in college track classes. Upon entering high school, she joined in a special college preparation program and was eventually accepted into UCLA, her first–choice college. Once at UCLA, she was again identified as

ESL and was invited to attend the UCLA Freshman Summer Program, a "bridge" program designed to prepare underrepresented or economically disadvantaged students for college-level work. She credits this program, with its adjunct ESL component, as having contributed significantly to her retention at the university. Martha is currently a sophomore majoring in kinesiology, and hopes to attend medical school upon graduation from UCLA.

Ana: Ana came to Los Angeles from El Salvador in 1979, at the age of twelve. With her came her mother, who was a seamstress, and her older brother—the father having abandoned the family at some earlier time. Like many other Salvadoran refugees, the three were undocumented. Ana began her education in the United States in fifth grade; she was in bilingual and ESL classes for the first three years of her stay here. In her junior high, the majority of students were Latinos, and her teachers emphasized Latino heritage. It wasn't until high school, where many of her friends were taking college preparatory classes, that Ana gained enough confidence to enroll in these classes herself.

Ana attributes her decision to attend college to her friends rather than her family; her mother encouraged her to get a trade, such as selling real estate, and to contribute to the family income. Knowing that her mother would disapprove, Ana applied to college secretly and informed her mother that she'd done so only after she had been admitted and had received notice of financial aid. On entry at UCLA, Ana was still undocumented, though she and her family members have since obtained permanent resident status.

At UCLA, Ana attended Freshman Summer Program and was identified as ESL—a fact which came as a shock to her. After taking the two quarters of ESL required of her, she subsequently took two additional ESL courses in order to improve her language skills. Now twenty-one, Ana is a junior majoring in Spanish literature and Latin American studies. She has recently found employment in an elementary school as a bilingual aide working with Latin American immigrant children. After graduation, she intends to be a bilingual teacher, teaching part time so that she can pursue graduate studies in social work. Though she speaks with an accent, Ana is extremely fluent in English; however, she claims that her oral Spanish is superior and prefers to speak in Spanish whenever possible.

Eileen: Born into a wealthy, educated Taiwanese family, Eileen was brought up by her maternal grandparents. When she was thirteen, her parents sent her to live with an aunt in Pennsylvania. She was one of only three Chinese students in her high school and knew only the English alphabet on arrival. She didn't mix freely with the native English-speaking students who, though polite to her, kept their distance and didn't make her feel welcome. Consequently, during her first three years in the United States she spoke almost exclusively Chinese. A highly motivated student, Eileen convinced the school to allow her to enroll in an honors English class while concurrently enrolled in an ESL class; she believes that the challenge of the honors class was an important factor in her language acquisition. Since her parents were still in Taiwan, Eileen bonded strongly with her English and Art teachers at high school, both of whom gave her lots of encouragement.

Upon Eileen's graduation from high school, her parents, who had recently moved from Taiwan to Pennsylvania, decided to move to California in order to become part of a larger Chinese-speaking community. Eileen knew that her parents expected her to attend a university, and she applied for admission to colleges on the east coast. One of these colleges offered her a scholarship, but her parents preferred to have Eileen move to California with them. This transition was difficult for her, but she agreed to apply to UCLA, where she was accepted. Now a junior admitted to the Honors Program, Eileen has a double major in English and microbiology. She is unsure of her future occupational plans because her own desire to be an English teacher conflicts with her parents' desire for her to attend medical school. She is working as a residential assistant in a university dorm and reports mixing with both Chinese and native English-speaking friends. She is highly fluent in English, both written and oral, and is comfortable in both languages.

Alex: Alex, also a Taiwanese immigrant, entered the United States in 1981 at the age of fourteen with his mother and younger brother. He attended a largely Anglo high school in Torrance, California, starting in the ninth grade. Because his high school had no ESL classes his first year, Alex was initially placed in regular English. It wasn't until his second year that the school instituted a program and he received ESL instruction. To compensate for the lack of ESL the first year, the school required him to attend two periods of ESL in tenth grade. In eleventh grade Alex was mainstreamed. During his senior year of high school, Alex took three English classes—a state of affairs which came about because the UC system at the time required four years of regular English from all college applicants, and Alex was determined to attend UCLA. He received a grade of A in all these courses, but he feels the grades didn't reflect his true proficiency, which he estimates was much lower.

On entry into UCLA's Freshman Summer Program, Alex was designated ESL and took the one course required of him. However, during his freshman year, Alex dropped out of UCLA due to academic problems; on reentering the university he decided that he needed to improve his language skills if he was to succeed. He thus enrolled in additional ESL and literature courses—including some upper-division courses in the English department. Today, although Alex's oral English is accented, it is highly idiomatic, and his writing displays few nonnative markers. Despite his fluency in English and his reports of mixing languages even when he speaks with his brother, Alex feels linguistic and cultural affinity with other Chinese speakers. Alex is a graduating senior in engineering and has been accepted to graduate school at UC Berkeley.

Ingrid: Ingrid first came to the United States from El Salvador in 1981 at the age of eleven. Sent by their college-educated parents to escape the political situation in their country, she and her sister stayed with Spanish-speaking relatives in Virginia. Ingrid was reluctant to speak any English during her first three months but gradually gained confidence and began speaking the new language. During this period, Ingrid spent many hours alone since her relatives worked long hours and her sister attended a different school. She feels that she matured a lot during this period spent without friends, and she attributes her English fluency to the many hours she spent alone watching television. She does not give much credit to the ESL pull-out classes taught by one of the nuns at the Catholic school. After a nine-month stay in the United States, Ingrid and her sister returned to El Salvador due to improved political conditions there.

At age sixteen, Ingrid returned to the United States with her eleven-year-old brother. Reluctant to leave El Salvador because she had bonded strongly with her high school peers there, she had a very negative attitude toward the United States: she blamed the United States for many of El Salvador's problems. Her initial re-entry experiences reinforced her negative feelings. Since she had missed fall enrollment at the local high school, she was placed instead in adult school and suffered from inappropriate placement in vocational classes. She recalls this experience as a nightmare. Once enrolled in high school, Ingrid was placed in ESL classes, which she did not find particularly challenging. Ingrid and her brother were later joined by the rest of the family, who had made the decision to emigrate.

Ingrid's determination to attend college appears to have been the result of both parental expectations and the encouragement that she received from a high school English teacher. Like several of the other students in this study, Ingrid attended the UCLA Freshman Summer Program. Currently she is a sociology major, tutors English in the university's Academic Advancement Program, and is unsure about her future career plans. Her English is accented but highly fluent, and her writing is very sophisticated.

Sin: Sin, an ethnic Chinese from Cambodia, entered the United States in 1979 at the age of ten. He and the eighteen members of his extended family (five siblings, parents, and other close relatives) were brought to the United States through the sponsorship of a Catholic priest. At first, they lived in Baltimore, in the church building. Here, Sin began fourth grade in a local elementary school, where he reports being happy and mixing freely with native speakers of English. During this period, he had semi-private tutoring in English and stayed an extra period after school for this purpose. He also reports watching television for extended periods of time. Some time later, the family moved to Texas, where Sin attended middle school and high school.

Though he was initially designated ESL, Sin requested to be allowed to take basic English, and in high school he attended honors English classes. During his senior year in high school the family moved to California, leaving Sin behind to finish high school. He was working at the time in the high school counseling office and received much encouragement from the counselor to take college preparatory courses and apply to college. UCLA was Sin's last choice, as he wanted to attend an Ivy League college, but his verbal English scores prevented him from being accepted there. He attended the UCLA Freshman Summer Program, and in his freshman year continued in a support program with an intensive writing component designed for high-risk freshmen. Now twenty-one, he is a premed student at UCLA. He speaks English with his sisters and brothers and with his roommates; though all the roommates are Asian, they share only English as a common language.

Carlos: At the age of seven, Carlos emigrated from Puerto Rico to Los Angeles with his Puerto Rican mother and Salvadoran father. After the father, a fisherman, had suffered a serious accident while working in Puerto Rico, he decided to pull up roots and move to Los Angeles to become an electrician. Carlos grew up in East L.A., living in housing projects where he was surrounded by drugs, crime, and violence. Since he had been enrolled in third grade in Puerto Rico, he was allowed to enter fourth grade here after having attended summer school. He reports knowing no English except the words *sofa* and *table* on entry, but he recalls picking up the language very rapidly. During his first year in the Los Angeles area, Carlos was grouped with other Spanish speakers, but otherwise he received no ESL instruction throughout his elementary and secondary career. His friends in East L.A. were largely Spanish-speaking, but Carlos reports using English as his primary language of communication.

In high school, Carlos's teachers encouraged him, and his high school appears to have had an active college recruiting program. Carlos reports frequenting the high school College Corner, browsing through college catalogs and participating in tours of college campuses. Carlos's decision to attend college seems to stem from the high school support system and from his own deep-rooted curiosity to learn; he reports that his parents neither encouraged nor discouraged him from pursuing higher education, though they voiced some concern about whether he would continue to contribute to the family income.

Once Carlos could demonstrate that he had received financial aid, the family placed no further barriers in his way. Like many of the other students, Carlos also attended the Freshman Summer Program, and for the first time in his life was required to take ESL coursework. He took three ESL courses before enrolling in the regular freshman composition course required of all engineering majors. Now a fourth-year student at UCLA, he is a materials engineering major and tutors math for the university's Academic Advancement Program. At home, he speaks English with his two sisters and uses Spanish primarily to communicate with his limited-English-speaking parents. At the university, he mixes with individuals from all ethnic backgrounds; nonetheless, he characterizes his own English as "Spanglish" and identifies heavily with his East L.A. and Puerto Rican roots.

Mylinh: Mylinh, an ethnic Chinese from Vietnam, fled her native country in 1979 at the age of nine, escaping by boat along with nine of her siblings. Her parents and two younger siblings stayed behind and at the time of the interview were still living in Vietnam. During a one-year stay in Hong Kong, while they waited to find a sponsor for their entrance into the United States, Mylinh attended ESL classes with students of differing ages and proficiency levels. Subsequently, she accompanied her older brothers and sisters to Portland, Oregon, where she entered fourth grade. Here she was placed in mixed ESL classes, which she attended for two years. Because of her age and the level of proficiency she attained, she was allowed to skip sixth grade and enter seventh grade, where she was mainstreamed.

Mylinh moved to California because a sister and her husband had found work in Los Angeles. Mylinh accompanied this sister, and entered junior high school in the area. Later, the other members of her family joined them in Los Angeles. Despite the fact that her parents had no education, in their letters from Vietnam they encouraged her to study hard and to pursue a higher education. In contrast, her high school counselors and even her siblings in California discouraged her from applying to UCLA. Mylinh did so nonetheless because she had heard about UCLA even before coming to California, and because many of her friends were applying there. As she explains it, this strong desire to attend a "name" college also stemmed from her concern that people not look down on her as a Vietnamese refugee. Mylinh is a premed student at UCLA, and is currently a junior. She is dominant in English and has minimal written Vietnamese, though she speaks Vietnamese with many of her friends. Because her roommates speak a variety of Asian languages, they communicate in English. Mylinh's written and spoken English display typical ESL markers.

David: In 1985, David came to Claremont, California from South Korea at the age of eighteen. His father, a professor of American Studies in South Korea, settled his family in the United States so that the children could obtain the benefits of an American education. He subsequently returned to Korea to continue his career and rejoins the family during the summer months only. David's immediate family in the

United States consists of his mother, a former professor of music who currently teaches piano, and two younger brothers. He entered high school as a junior; he reports having been ahead there in all subjects but English, since the educational level of the Korean high school which he attended was higher than that in the United States.

At the U.S. high school he was initially placed in ESL despite previous English instruction in Korea but later took an exam and was able to join regular composition and American literature classes. In these, he reports that he struggled but received decent grades. Attending college was not so much a personal decision as a family expectation, and David's first choice of college was an Ivy League school. However, the family preferred that he stay in California, and thus he applied to a number of the more prestigious private colleges in Southern California. UCLA, the only school which admitted him, was his last choice.

Invited to attend UCLA's Freshman Summer Program, David accepted and was identified as ESL. He took two quarters of ESL coursework and then satisfied his composition requirement through the regular English program. David is currently majoring in chemical engineering and plans to enter a Ph.D. program when he graduates. David's next younger brother is a premed student at UCLA; the other brother is still in high school but intends to attend UCLA as well. David is quite reluctant to engage in conversation in English; despite good writing skills in English, he says that he is still Korean-dominant. He associates primarily with other Koreans and adheres strongly to Korean culture.

Emerging from our interviews is the overwhelming impression that these students share very little other than their identity as nonnative speakers of English. As we look at their backgrounds, we note, for example, that there is a wide range of formal exposure to English: some of the students (David and Mylinh) received English instruction prior to coming to the United States; others had varying amounts and types of ESL instruction during their elementary and secondary schooling, and two (Carlos and Sin) had no formal ESL instruction outside of tutoring prior to university entrance.

A similar range is evidenced in these students' informal exposure to English. Several students note that extensive interactions with English speakers and television viewing have been major influences in their acquisition of English, while others (Ana and David) note that they remain uncomfortable in an English-speaking environment and avoid any unnecessary contact with the English language. Yet others (for example, Martha) report that they felt more comfortable in certain domains with their home language and more comfortable in others with English.

Nor were attitudes toward learning English, often thought to be a highly influential factor in successful learning, particularly uniform. Although most of these students recognized the importance of English for academic success, they did not always see English as socially important. Evidence of these students' determination to maintain their home languages is found in the balanced bilinguals Ingrid and Martha and in the fact that two of the students (Ana and

David), despite a long period of residence in the United States, still consider themselves non-English dominant. All these students work hard to maintain their home language.

In spite of all these differences in backgrounds, attitudes, and experiences, one factor did emerge as extremely important to all of these students: their motivation to succeed. Whether that motivation was the result of extrinsic pressures or whether it was purely intrinsic, it appears to be crucial to the students' success. In fact, awareness of the importance of motivation is evident in the unanimous advice that the students give to other students—in essence: Work hard on English in order to succeed at college; don't rely on anyone else; your success is up to you.

THE STUDENTS AT A GLANCE

Here, in chart form for easy reference, we summarize the ways in which the students compare with one another on a number of important issues.

Home Language

Spanish	Chinese	Cambodian	Korean	Vietnamese
Ana	Eileen	Sin	David	Mylinh
Ingrid	Sin			
Carlos	Alex			
Martha				

Parents' Formal Education

Preliterate	Primary	Secondary	University	Ph.D.
	Martha	Mylinh	B.A./B.S.	David
		Carlos	Ingrid	
		Ana	Eileen	
			Sin	

Self-Assessed Proficiency in English

1. Writing

Poor	Below Avg.	Average	Above Avg.	Excellent
	Mylinh	Sin	Carlos	Ingrid
		Ana	David	Eileen
			Martha	Alex

2. Speaking

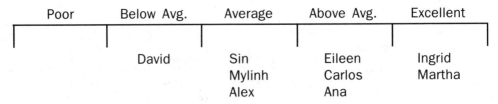

Poor	Below Avg.	Average	Above Avg.	Excellent
	David	Sin	Eileen	Ingrid
		Mylinh	Carlos	Martha
		Alex	Ana	

Contact with Native Speakers

1. In High School

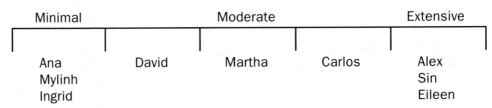

Minimal		Moderate		Extensive
Ana	David	Martha	Carlos	Alex
Mylinh				Sin
Ingrid				Eileen

2. At the University

Minimal		Moderate		Extensive
Alex	Mylinh	Sin		Carlos
Ana	David	Ingrid		Eileen
		Martha		

Amount of ESL/EFL Instruction

1. Prior to Arrival in the United States

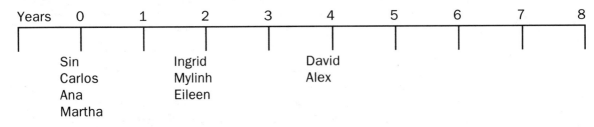

Years	0	1	2	3	4	5	6	7	8
	Sin		Ingrid		David				
	Carlos		Mylinh		Alex				
	Ana		Eileen						
	Martha								

2. Prior to University Entrance

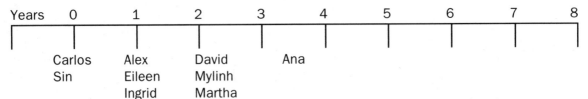

Years	0	1	2	3	4	5	6	7	8
	Carlos	Alex	David	Ana					
	Sin	Eileen	Mylinh						
		Ingrid	Martha						

3. At the University

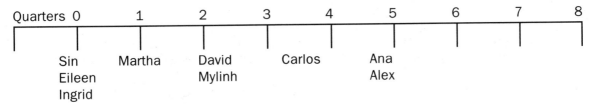

Quarters 0   1   2   3   4   5   6   7   8

Sin — Martha — David — Carlos — Ana
Eileen   Mylinh   Alex
Ingrid

Language Dominance

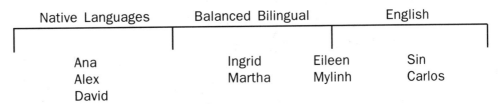

Native Languages	Balanced Bilingual		English
Ana Alex David	Ingrid Martha	Eileen Mylinh	Sin Carlos

Attitude toward ESL Instruction in High School

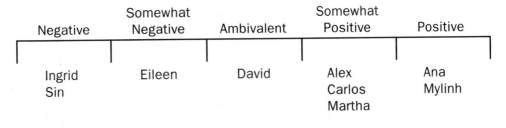

Negative	Somewhat Negative	Ambivalent	Somewhat Positive	Positive
Ingrid Sin	Eileen	David	Alex Carlos Martha	Ana Mylinh

Motivation

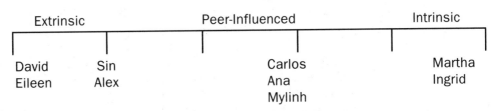

Extrinsic		Peer-Influenced		Intrinsic
David Eileen	Sin Alex		Carlos Ana Mylinh	Martha Ingrid

THE STUDENTS AS LANGUAGE LEARNERS: THEIR OWN WORDS

In our interviews, the students had much to say about their attitudes toward themselves as learners and users of language. We were particularly interested in what they had to say in relation to issues often discussed in studies of successful language learners: their feelings about contact with native speakers, their language dominance, their attitudes toward ESL and bilingual instruction.[1]

Feelings about Contact with Native Speakers

Several students felt that though they were surrounded by native speakers, they had very little interaction with them. Martha, who entered elementary school in an all-Anglo community, expressed feelings of isolation and alienation:

> It was really bad because . . . I was almost the only one . . . and there were no translators, so I was just sitting there and they were speaking English to me and I didn't understand anything . . . I was isolated, just by myself.

Similarly, David noted that he did not seek contact with Caucasians, and even felt estranged from American-born Korean students. Ana, who represents a somewhat extreme case of this sentiment, still feels discriminated against and distances herself from English speakers.

> I think most Caucasians and I don't have anything in common . . . and I know it's bad to say but I think some of them, most of them are prejudiced. And I have this with my skin color and I think it's just my background of when I was small, how they used to pick on my skin color.

Other students mentioned having had native English-speaking friends at certain points in their life but not at others. Eileen, who attended an all-Anglo high school, felt herself very much an outsider during this period of her life but now mixes easily and often with her English-speaking peers. So does Martha, today. Conversely, Sin feels that his acquisition of English was strongly influenced by his childhood native-speaking friend Herbert (as well as by his addiction to American television) but reports associating primarily with other Asians at the university. And Alex, who feels totally isolated from native speakers of English at the university, recalls with fond memories the assistance he got from native English-speaking peers in high school:

> At high school, everybody is buddy buddy. Doesn't matter if your English is poor, fine, we help you out, we'll bail you out, and basically language was not a problem. At least I didn't recognize language as a problem and neither did most of my friends.

Yet others, such as Carlos, indicate that they mix freely with all races and ethnicities, native and nonnative speaking, and feel no estrangement whatsoever.

Language Dominance

Regarding the issue of language dominance, there is again little uniformity among the students we interviewed. In spite of what now amounts to many years of attending school in English, the language dominance patterns of these nine students vary widely. Mylinh, for example, follows the familiar pattern of language loss, having left her native Vietnam at age nine before acquiring first-language literacy skills. She reports having lost all her Chinese language skills and many of her Vietnamese skills as well, especially those used in writing. A similar case is that of Sin, who assesses himself as completely English-dominant.

> For me I think [my language dominance] it's English, because English is my first written language. . . . And I never had schooling before, Chinese or Cambodian, so this English is my first real language that I go to school to learn. . . . Because Chinese, when you get to a deeper language I couldn't understand it. I just speak the . . . you know, everyday . . . dialect.

Not surprisingly, these students report using English to communicate even with friends who, like themselves, have an Asian language background. As Mylinh notes:

> When I have to express, it's easier [in English]. In Vietnamese, its harder for me to express myself.

Yet others assess themselves as balanced bilinguals. Ingrid and Martha, for example, feel that they have managed to maintain their native Spanish while acquiring fluency in English; they value their bilingualism highly. Martha recounts how as a child she resented her mother's insistence that they speak Spanish at home but now appreciates her language heritage:

> My mom never wanted us to speak English at home. She didn't want us to forget the language and [I spoke] Spanish with my brother. Always . . . Well, back then I used to think— I want to speak English with my brother . . . but my mother would get mad . . . now I'm glad because at least I didn't forget my language. . . . I appreciate that I know two languages, and read in them.

At the far end of the continuum are students such as David and Ana, who see themselves as native-language dominant—both linguistically and culturally. Both of these students report using English only in their university classes; otherwise they avoid speaking English. Ana emphatically states her preference for Spanish:

> I will only speak English if I have to . . . I can express myself better in Spanish. I can get madder better in Spanish and be happier. It's from the heart, I think.

Martha, on the other hand, finds that her use of English or Spanish depends on the context or situation in which she finds herself. In Martha's world, Spanish is the language of the heart (as it is with Ana), while English represents the voice of authority:

> In some things like emotional things, I think I express myself better in Spanish . . . and in English, it's more—not cold and

sour, and whatever—but when it comes to love things, expressing emotions that kind of hard to do, I do them better in Spanish, and then music and everything, I think in Spanish. . . . If I go shopping, or whatever, or something goes wrong . . . I would just notice myself speaking English. When it comes to being authoritative, English is my language.

Attitudes toward ESL and Bilingual Instruction

These nine students we interviewed have experienced a variety of ESL and bilingual treatments. Some were placed immediately upon entry in all-English classes and forced to fend for themselves. Carlos and Sin, both of whom arrived when they were elementary-school age, were placed in regular classrooms and had minimal ESL tutoring only. Martha, who entered kindergarten in the United States, had no ESL instruction until her first year of junior high, where she then attended ESL classes for a full academic year. Ana experienced two years of bilingual education in elementary school and was mainstreamed in junior high. Mylinh, Ingrid, David, Alex, and Eileen all had some EFL instruction prior to coming to the United States. But again, their experiences upon arriving in the United States differed widely: Alex, Eileen, and Ingrid had minimal ESL pull-out instruction prior to university entrance while David and Mylinh were part of a formal ESL class.

At the university, experiences also differed. Carlos, despite having been mainstreamed throughout elementary and secondary school, tested into UCLA's next-to-lowest level of ESL proficiency and was shocked to find himself enrolled in ESL classes—an experience which he later acknowledged benefited him greatly:

> I felt kinda bad, I thought that I knew how to write and stuff, but I guess I didn't. But then I go, well I need the help. My writing is really bad.

Similar feelings are reported by Mylinh, Ana, Martha, and David—all of whom were initially surprised and even upset to find themselves placed in university-level ESL classes since they had been mainstreamed in the Los Angeles area schools they had attended. Martha notes:

> Oh, I remember they told us and I was so—I am going to cry— it's happening again. . . . So we get into a group and everybody in my group, I just started talking to them. . . . I just wanted to see their reaction—and everybody felt just the same . . . they made a mistake, they just want to fill people in the classes.

Unlike these students, Sin, Eileen, and Ingrid managed to negotiate their way out of university ESL courses despite being told by counselors or faculty members that they were in need of this instruction. They were reluctant to take ESL classes because they wanted the challenge of being in a "regular" class. Because of their identified developmental writing characteristics, however, all these students were enrolled in special intensive sections of freshman composition—sections where they received additional hours of instruction and more individualized attention from their writing instructors.

Not surprisingly, given this variety of formal language learning experiences, the students' attitudes toward bilingual and ESL instruction differ widely. Ana is particularly grateful for the bilingual education she received when she first arrived in the United States. According to her, not only was she given the chance to maintain her native language, but she also had an opportunity to study her native culture:

> Certain days of the week . . . we went to this other teacher . . . we only speak Spanish. We learn about Columbus and our background, like Indian background or things we would have learned if we would have been in our own country, you know, so not to neglect those kind of thing. I think it was a pretty positive impression.

Other students, such as Sin, Eileen, and Ingrid, are less positively inclined toward the ESL instruction they have received—and even express worry about the stigma that may be attached to the label "ESL." In Ingrid's words:

> The ESL classes in our schools don't have a challenging curriculum, most of it. . . . It's . . . giving you . . . books that have the big print and stuff like that for you to read . . . it had a bad connotation in high school. ESL was the low track level, people look down on you when you're taking ESL.

While these students don't have positive feelings about ESL instruction, David and Mylinh disagree, noting that ESL classes made them feel comfortable due to their supportive atmosphere and the close bonds they formed to other students in the same linguistic boat. In David's words:

> Those ESL classes were set up like family atmosphere. So everybody just feel free to speak and feel free to express themselves—not as the regular classes because those regular class, classmates like feel different from there. So we felt kind of unity in the ESL classes.

Finally, Alex and Martha, who initially had a negative attitude toward ESL classes, had a change of heart once they experienced university ESL classes. Martha, who originally was dismayed to be placed in an ESL class when she had been mainstreamed all through high school, provides the following testimonial to her university ESL class: "I realized how little I knew after I took the class. So I did need it. I was happy that I took it." And Alex, who experienced difficulties after college entrance due to his limited command of English, was forced to drop out of the university. On his return, he enrolled in every available ESL class:

> I thought about it, I figure, hey, the main, the language at United States is English. If I don't know English, I cannot go anywhere. If I don't, even I know my technical stuff real well,

the best I will do is—I'll be stuck in front of some kind of computer crap in a lab in the basement of a building and be a high tech technician all my life. There's no way. I, so I figured it's not the way to go. And maybe I give English a shot.

MOTIVATION AND ITS SOURCES

Not surprisingly, the students we interviewed are all highly motivated; however, they are highly motivated for very different reasons. Some are motivated extrinsically—for example, by parental pressure. David is a classic example of the student who has been pushed to succeed by his parents.

> During my first year here, I work pretty hard. My Dad help me, also. . .he forced me to memorize the, all those vocabularies like uh 20 or 30 words per day and during the weekend like, I guess several hundred words like uh review the total thing. And he made us to write diary in English.

Eileen is another example of the student whose college career is controlled by her parent's expectations of her:

> I never knew there's a decision to be made, I mean because I knew I, I'm gonna go to college. See, the family I came from is . . . like a very high class . . . we're pretty wealthy and pretty well off and so I guess when you have a little bit like money then they assume that your children are in college.

For students from the lower socioeconomic stratum such as Ana, Martha, and Carlos, the drive to succeed comes largely from within themselves. Some, like Martha and Ana, had to convince their mothers to be allowed to seek a higher education. Martha recounts:

> What did my mother think? . . . She's a housekeeper, so that is all that she knows . . . So I would want to talk to her and she wouldn't understand . . . oh, she goes, you're aiming too high . . . you can't do that . . . you're in another country. She wanted me to be passive and just settle with whatever. We'll get you some housekeeping jobs.

Given the lack of a parental support system, these students had to seek ways to support themselves financially throughout their studies. As Carlos says:

> Well my father, he wanted me to work so I could help him with the rent, house stuff like that . . . Yeah, I told him that . . . once I get my degree then I'll be able to help him out and stuff . . . I wanna better myself, you know, more knowledge . . . Yeah, I always liked it . . . I always liked to learn things.

Students in high schools that did not have strong college preparatory programs had to rely on peer support or their own initiative to receive information about college entrance requirements. Mylinh notes that she had to fend for herself applying to college: "In my school, everyone on their own. We get information from friends."

IMPLICATIONS FOR EDUCATORS

The Students' Advice to Peers

Perhaps the most interesting responses in our interviews came in answer to the question "What advice would you give to nonnative high school students wishing to attend college?" For a start, they advise that students take maximum advantage of their time at high school. This includes taking Advanced Placement (AP) classes and using the high school years to hone their English language skills before having to deal with the linguistic demands of higher education. Sin suggests:

> I think . . . if you want to improve your English, the best time is before you come to college. Because when you come to college, you know, you don't have that much time to read or write. You have to write, but you don't have time to develop it. So the best time is in high school . . . try to read a lot and . . . practice writing . . . try to take those higher courses where they make you write.

Alex echoes Sin's words with some heartfelt advice:

> College dues are hefty, they charge interest too! I got my grades to show you . . . You want to get the language, linguistic barrier, out of the way as early as possible. . . . So if you don't get the problem solved at high school level you're going to have one hell of tough time at college level . . . the axe is going to fall on you sooner or later, I mean the longer you put it off the worse it's going to get.

The students also stressed the importance of self-initiative in pursuing academic goals. Ana advises high school students:

> I think you follow your own instincts. It's not like teachers were that helpful overall. Even the counselor was not that helpful. . . . It was not they look for you, you look for them. Once you look for them they will be looking for you. Then, I mean, it went the other way around. But it was only you who wanted to go to college. It was you who had to know what to do, when to do it, and how to do it.

Martha and Eileen have advice along similar lines for university students. Eileen notes:

> The problem of university is . . . that you have to go out and look for opportunities yourself. Nothing, nothing ever like just hit you . . . when you're walking or something. It just doesn't happen in this college. And you have to be very aggressive, and you have to be very independent, you have to be very outgoing. That's how you have to be, that's how you succeed in a really big college like UCLA. And I learn that the really hard way.

The Students' Advice to Teachers

Students were less specific in their advice to teachers. Nonetheless, they had strong feelings about the teachers they had experienced in their elementary and secondary years—both positive and negative feelings. Thus, the advice we synthesize here comes indirectly out of the comments they made about their teachers, counselors, and high school curricula.

Several students expressed distrust of teachers who were not members of their ethnic group and felt that those teachers discounted their abilities. While some were aided in their college applications by their high school counselors, others felt that they were discouraged from applying to the university. Ingrid, for example, comments on the stark difference between the encouragement she received in her native country and the way in which her United States teachers viewed her:

> I was very encouraged in El Salvador and I didn't like the fact that I was discouraged here. I was discouraged to go to college. I was discouraged to take college course classes. . . . It was my initiative to say, "these are the courses that I want to take" . . . nobody was telling me, "look, you have the potential to take these courses."

Even those who were encouraged felt that their inner-city schools had not adequately prepared them for the demands of the university, even in their Advanced Placement courses. Martha compares the academic preparation her inner-city school provided her with the preparation some of her college friends had received in more affluent school districts:

> My high school, particularly my high school I think, is very deprived. When I got here, I thought, well, high school was great, they taught me everything. I came here, I didn't know anything in chemistry. Physics, I had AP Physics, I realized I knew nothing because for some reason all our high school

teachers don't rely on books. . . . I mean I
friends, they had books, they had tests, they ha
understand, do the problems. . . . Just like here.

On the more positive side, some students were very
who had taken a personal interest in them and pushed then
for example, notes that his biology teacher repeatedly told h
potential to succeed. And Eileen comments on her particularly
with two of her teachers:

My English teacher and my art teacher are like my best friends
in high school, it's really ironic because, I mean my parents
aren't here so I form . . . friends with my teachers.

LOOKING TO THE FUTURE

If motivation seems to be the key to success in higher education and if it
operates in the face of varying life and school experiences, what can we surmise
about our role as teachers? What can we do to aid nonnative students and help
them achieve their goals? As we have seen, the students we interviewed were
already highly self-motivated, and that motivation may be the product of
psychological and social forces over which teachers have little control. However,
we do believe that the students' comments can guide us as teachers of language
minority students by providing us with methods of nurturing motivation where
it already exists and of cultivating it where it does not.

One thing that teachers of language minority students can do is to stress
the role that language plays in academic success. Helping students to reach this
understanding early in the language acquisition process is critical, and several
of the students we interviewed—Alex and Sin, for example—expressed regret at
not having attended more to their English language skills during their formative
educational years.

Perhaps even more importantly, teachers should understand that many
nonnative speakers view our emphasis on English language and American
culture as a negation of the values of their own culture and language. Thus we
must take care in the language curriculum to value our students' cultural and
linguistic heritage, and we should encourage students to retain their own
language and culture while learning English. We can try to achieve this aim by
using materials that recognize the multilingual, multicultural nature of our
student population and by selecting activities and readings in which students
can see themselves and the issues they face validated.

As mentioned above, the students indicated that they often felt a lack of
understanding on the part of some teachers and lacked appropriate role models.
Clearly, there is a need for stronger minority role models on all faculties.
However, as teachers of any ethnic group, we can help meet our students' needs
by becoming more sensitive to their cultures. We can do this by becoming

nowledgeable about the culture of the student population in the classroom, by discussing cultural differences in class, and by increasing our contact with individual students as much as circumstances allow.

The students we interviewed sometimes felt that their teachers and counselors discounted their overall intellectual abilities because they did not have nativelike command of English. Sometimes we need to look beyond surface errors to recognize the strong points a speaker or writer is making. We all sometimes fall into the trap of making judgments based on looks, dress, or language. As teachers, we must remember that students adjusting to a new culture, language, and country may not exhibit the same skills as native-born students. However, we must not let their temporary difficulties deprive them of opportunities to succeed in the future. Talking with students about their own goals and plans and helping them work to fulfill their dreams and ambitions will aid students to make realistic choices about their futures.

THE GREATEST NEED: MENTORING

The students we interviewed seemed particularly receptive to the assistance they had received from trusted teachers, academic counselors, and peer tutors. Providing mentor systems and role models for students is one means of shoring up the support system for language minority students. Mentors can come from the faculty, from peers, from local colleges or universities, or from the general community. Here are some ways to set up a mentoring program:

- School districts can set up teacher/student mentor programs in which teachers develop personal relations with students based on shared interests or cultural heritage. These mentors would discuss students' future plans, mediate conflicts they are experiencing (i.e., classroom difficulties, conflicts between home and school), and simultaneously serve as role models and trusted confidantes.

- Similarly, schools can set up peer mentoring and tutoring programs in which older students serve as mentors and role models for younger students. Again, matching students of similar ethnic and cultural backgrounds is one promising model for such a system. However, there are also advantages to pairing native speakers with nonnative speakers since this can help break down the strong ethnic barriers that exist in many schools today.

- Outreach programs from colleges and universities are a third means by which high school students can be motivated to think of themselves as college material. In such a program, local students in higher education are recruited to visit high school classes and share their personal experiences in getting to college and succeeding there. As these students discuss the barriers they have overcome, high school students can identify and see new possibilities for themselves.

- Peer letter writing is a good technique for establishing contact between individual students as well as improving English language skills. In this mentoring system, students are matched randomly; they correspond rather than interact in a face-to-face manner, often never coming in contact with their correspondents. Letter writing can be set up between classes in a given school, or between institutions (e.g., the high school and the junior high school; a college and a high school).

- Finally, language minority students often lack professional role models in the outside community. Here again, high schools can invite successful members of the minority community to visit language minority classrooms. In addition to talking to classes in the school, these individuals can further serve as mentors by providing students with opportunities to visit off-campus sites and to explore careers in the field. This may lead to the establishment of internships or field studies programs. The Puente Program of the Bay Area Writing Project in California is one promising model for a long-term mentoring program using several of these possibilities.

We believe that perhaps the most important contribution we can make to future students' success is to recognize and foster the power of personal motivation. This often allows the seemingly most unlikely student to overcome hardships and obstacles and succeed in higher education. As teachers, we need to urge students to pursue loftier goals, and to push them as necessary. With our encouragement and support, students can see that they have a chance, that they can succeed in higher education in spite of language, cultural, or financial obstacles—assuming, of course, that they want to succeed badly enough. Ultimately, raising this awareness in our students may be the most important contribution we can make to their education.

NOTES

1. See, for example, Rubin (1975); Naiman, Frohlich, Stern, and Todesco (1978); Politzer and McGroarty (1985); Schumann (1986); Brown, (1987); McLaughlin (1987); Reid (1987); Trueba (1987; 1989); and Skehan (1989).

SHELTERED INSTRUCTION ACROSS THE DISCIPLINES: SUCCESSFUL TEACHERS AT WORK

Linda Sasser ■ *Beth Winningham*

When visitors enter Janeane Vigliotti's classroom, they immediately notice a difference between this world history classroom and others they may have visited. The students are seated in teams of four or five, their heads drawn close together as they intently discuss an aspect of the lesson that the teacher has asked them to focus on. As they work, Janeane moves from cluster to cluster, asking questions, confirming and praising student ideas, effectively checking with all members of the class in six or seven brief stops.

On the bulletin boards are samples of student projects—drawings, maps, written descriptions. Two large plastic-coated maps have been pulled down beside the chalkboard, and on the front board is today's agenda. Class opened with an interactive review of yesterday's lesson, moved on to a brief lecture presenting new material and then to a filmstrip during which students took notes on the visual presentation of material they had been introduced to in the teacher's lecture.

Now, in groups, the students are involved in comparing their lecture notes with the filmstrip material. Each group is collating its responses on a matrix; lively discussion arises as each team decides which ideas belong in which categories. The maps, textbooks, and classroom reference books (particularly an atlas) are being used as references to help clarify points of discussion. In a few minutes, a representative from each team of students will report their discussion to the whole class. As they report the answers to their guiding questions, Janeane will use an overhead projector and a transparency of the matrix they have worked on to record the ideas of each group for all to see. As the students continue their discussion, visitors hear a mix of languages, as well as English, for this class is a special sheltered section of world history for limited English proficient students (LEP students).

Though the course outline for Janeane Vigliotti's sheltered world history includes the same intellectually demanding content as a regular mainstream course, this class differs in significant ways from an unsheltered counterpart. In sheltered courses, instructors use a series of instructional strategies derived in

part from second-language-acquisition methodology. English i
instruction, but the curriculum and materials are modified
English proficient students comprehensible access to cognit
ideas and concepts.

High schools with large language minority populations
within these populations are intelligent, alert, and dedicated
fluent English speakers, whose success depends upon obtaining
contained in a curriculum taught in a language they do not fully comprehend. The question becomes how to teach them. The best answer, of course, would be to offer instruction through the primary language until English language proficiency catches up with students' academic proficiency. The next-best answer is through sheltered instruction.

Via the techniques of sheltered instruction, cognitively demanding and context-reduced activities can be made more comprehensible by embedding the concepts in a context, thus enabling students to deal with challenging academic subject matter despite their limited proficiency in English. Teachers should recall at all times that limited English speakers in secondary school are *not cognitively limited*. The purpose of sheltered classrooms is to deliver the concepts essential to the course in a way appropriate to the students' English language development.

Sheltered content classes are intended for students who have attained intermediate fluency in English. They have acquired the listening and speaking skills to permit them to understand questions and to answer orally. Inter-mediate-fluency students speak predominantly in complete sentences and use a wide range of vocabulary; they have emerging English-literacy skills and are capable of carrying on a discussion or producing an extended narrative.

Carrying both graduation and university preparation credit, sheltered classes have evolved as a means of linking the curriculum goals of the school with a philosophy that facilitates meeting the language needs and life goals of intelligent and diligent students. Without sheltered classes, many urban high schools could offer little but failure to many limited English proficient students.

HOW DO LANGUAGE MINORITY STUDENTS EXPERIENCE AMERICAN SCHOOLS?

Momentarily consider the secondary school environment as it must appear to an immigrant student—visualize the dense swarms of people in the cafeteria, the paper banners with their esoteric messages strung across hallways; hear the sharp, metallic slamming of locker doors, and listen to a cacaphony of cries, calls, and shouts in an unfamiliar language; sit in a classroom and listen to the teacher begin to speak in a language you only partially understand—and the need for sheltered instruction becomes readily apparent. Though native English speakers may also struggle to comprehend the concepts of the secondary school curriculum, the task is doubly difficult for LEP students. Raining in upon them, in a veritable storm of language, are new concepts embedded in various new contexts.

Academic success in high school requires the mastery of challenging and possibly unfamiliar *concepts*—as in the symbolic language of algebra or the theories of psychology. For some students, the notion that there may be several right answers (as in literary analysis) or no single path to a correct solution may be culturally unfamiliar or dismaying. These students will need assistance as they begin to reflect, express, and learn to defend their opinions in response to challenges from teachers and curriculum. This can be an enormous load of new information for students who may come to us with partial or interrupted schooling—for much of the American secondary school curriculum is predicated upon the assumption that students have previously been exposed to the metalanguage of literature, landmark events in the history of mankind from the vantage point of the United States, or basic scientific principles.

For example, in algebra, a student who understands the symbolic notation of $5c - b/3$ may not recognize the written operation expressed as five times c, decreased by one-third of b. Reflect on how much syntactic and semantic knowledge is required to solve a word problem like the following:

> If one number is four times as large as another number, and
> the smaller number is decreased by two, the result is fourteen
> less than the larger number. What are the two numbers?
> (Bobrow, 1985, p. 260)

To solve this problem, not only must the reader understand the role of logical connectors (*if, and*), comparative structures (*as . . . as, er* suffix), and passive voice (is decreased by), but they must also realize that *another number* and *the smaller number* represent the same quantity. Further consider how this question about "Rip Van Winkle" asks the student to draw upon familiarity with literary terminology as well as the larger context of United States history:

> At what period in American history does the story begin? At what
> period does the last episode take place? What are some of the
> great events that occurred in America while Rip was asleep?

A student who attempts to read "Rip Van Winkle" has to contend not only with the sometimes archaic language but with all the elements of a short story as well as the relatively sophisticated sociopolitical context.

In addition, the *context* for learning these concepts may be baffling or alien to a newcomer in American schools. Imagine a Central American, Pakistani, or Indochinese girl in a state-required health science course that covers human sexuality. Not only may the subject matter be something which her culture considers to be very personal and private, something which may be unmentioned even between women in her home culture, but in the American high school this information is presented openly, graphically, sometimes casually, and, possibly most difficult of all, in a class composed of both genders. When Khanh asks a question about birth control, her ESL teacher asks, "What did your health teacher tell you about it?" Khanh dips her head and responds so quietly that the teacher strains to hear, "I don't know. I was too embarrassed to listen."

The most obvious source of stress is the *language* of the academic classroom. Its complexities are clear in textbook sentences like the one that follows.

> The ichneumons, like most wasps, *generally* live *freely* as adults but pass their larval life as parasites *feeding* on the bodies of other animals, almost *invariably* members of their own phylum, Arthropoda.

Complex even for the native speaker, this example contains general and specialized scientific nomenclature, as well as modifiers that restrict and limit the description of wasp behavior. More than being a simple matter of content-specific vocabulary, the difficulties of academic English include many semantic shifts—that is, the meanings of words shift and alter so subtly that a word understood in one setting is puzzling in another. Think of a U.S. history course that refers to a system of "checks and balances," in which vocabulary familiar at the bank and market has been used to refer to the way this government is protected from an abuse of power by any one branch. Syntax, too, plays a part— the language of science is full of passive constructions: "the initial data *was collected* in two stages, spaced two days apart" or "raw total scores of correct answers by type *were analyzed*." Sentences in English can become enormously long and complex, clause after clause and multiple phrases serving to modify the central idea, as in the following example:

> Gabe shuffled back to them and sat down, leaning on his knees and looking at the floor between his feet, so all you could see was the swell of his big shoulders, like the shoulders of a walrus, and the top of his head with the hair matted and straw in it, and those tremendous, thick paws hanging limp between his knees. (Clark, 1940, pp. 42–43)

An LEP student encountering a sentence like the one above is like Theseus entering the maze beneath the palace of Crete—she'll need to follow a thread in order to reemerge unscathed.

SHELTERED CONTENT INSTRUCTION: A DESCRIPTION

For understanding the purpose of sheltered instruction, the umbrella is a useful metaphor. When limited English proficient students enter United States high schools, they encounter the unfamiliar elements we've just discussed. As an umbrella shelters pedestrians in a rain storm, so sheltered classes offer limited English proficient students some protection from the storm of concepts, contexts, and language, thus giving them the opportunity to attain concept goals and progress academically as they acquire English language proficiency.

Research on second language acquisition has greatly influenced methodology for teachers of limited English proficient students. Sheltered methodology, borrowed from ESL strategies, emphasizes the concept of *comprehensible input*—very simply, making concepts understood by the learner. This is accomplished through the use of the following:

- Real objects and materials (realia)
- Manipulatives (rods, attribute blocks and geo boards in mathematics)
- Visuals (study prints or textbook illustrations)
- Graphic organizers (matrices, Venn diagrams, semantic maps and webs)
- Planned opportunities for interaction between all individuals in the classroom

Though many classes for native English speakers may still present information almost exclusively through the teacher's lectures, in the sheltered classroom students are encouraged to *use their emerging English speaking skills to understand new ideas.* In both mainstream and sheltered content classes, the content class quite properly focuses on subject area concepts, yet native speakers of English will understand the flow of language from the instructor, leaving only the concepts to be acquired. In a sheltered class, however, the students are acquiring English language skills simultaneously with the concepts. Therefore, language cannot be the sole route to comprehension; rather, the meaning of the concepts must be made comprehensible through segmenting the information into linguistically more manageable portions and through the use of extralinguistic materials.

Further, teachers of sheltered classes *modify their own speech*, emphasizing vocabulary through critical pauses before key phrases, frequent restatements and paraphrases, and occasionally exaggerated intonation. These linguistic strategies cue limited English proficient listeners to listen intently. By interrupting the stream of language to check on students' comprehension, teachers of sheltered classes are able to assess the pace of instruction, slowing or repairing as needed. These comprehension checks occur through a variety of question types ranging from simple wh- types to higher-level critical thinking inquiries. The ability to modify instruction in these ways determines the effectiveness of a sheltered teacher like Ms. Vigliotti.

THEORY IN A NUTSHELL

The work of Jim Cummins (1981) has profoundly influenced methodology for all teachers of limited English proficient students by distinguishing between language used for social and academic purposes. Social language (BICS—basic interpersonal communication skills) is the language students use among themselves on the school campus and in the classroom. More critical to success in secondary and post-secondary programs, however, is academic language (CALP—cognitive academic language proficiency); CALP is the language of the secondary content-area classroom. Content-area language includes not only vocabulary specific to the course but also syntactic structures that must be understood and manipulated to achieve full comprehension. Limited English proficient students who develop only BICS will not advance in curricula that measure success through CALP. Secondary programs for limited English proficient students have two pathways to successful development of CALP: they can offer courses in the primary language of the students, or they can offer sheltered programs. Anything less targets LEP students for failure.

To make clear the distinction between BICS and CALP, Cummins has proposed that language uses be located on a quadrant with two axes. As Figure 2.1 illustrates, along the north/south axis is a line which extends from "cognitively undemanding" to "cognitively demanding." The distinction between these terms may be explained as the difference between subconscious control of the routines and patterns of everyday life (undemanding) and a conscious focus on understanding new concepts or materials (demanding).

Along the west/east axis of the quadrant is another line extending from "context embedded" to "context reduced." This line distinguishes between events or situations offering many clues that assist in the comprehension of language related to social events (facial expressions, gestures, and real objects)

Cognitively Undemanding

Getting an absence excuse
Buying popcorn
Oral instructions
Initial levels of ESL
Some content classes
   (art, music, P.E.)   **BICS**
 	
A
	Talking on the telephone
	Written instructions
	   without illustration
	
	C

Context Embedded	**Context Reduced**
B	D
Lab demonstrations/experiments A-V assisted lessons Basic math computations Plane geometry Projects & activities Health instruction	**CALP** Standardized tests Math concepts & applications in algebra Teacher lectures Social science texts Mainstream English texts Most content classes

Cognitively Demanding

(Adapted from Schifini, 1985, p. 4)

Figure 2.1. Illustration of Cummins's Grid

and those that offer few clues (an orchestra score, a textbook page, a calculus equation). The resulting quadrants in the figure are labeled A, B, C, D. Relatively easier language uses—those of rote or routine—can be located at top left in the quadrant.

According to Cummins, BICS fall in the A quadrant. Face-to-face interactions, like those required to get an excuse after an absence or to buy popcorn in the school canteen, become easily routinized and almost subconscious. Because these are everyday transactions and so heavily rooted in context, students in such interactions often "sound" as if they speak English well. However, events like telephone calls, which may also be cognitively undemanding yet relatively context reduced, might be placed in the C quadrant. Because a telephone conversation lacks paralinguistic clues to help the limited English speaker comprehend—there are no objects to gesture toward, no facial expressions to assist with understanding—the speaker's proficiency in English may seem much more limited. In the D quadrant lie the most difficult of all language events—those that are both cognitively demanding and context reduced. Functioning in this quadrant requires cognitive academic-language proficiency, for here are contained the teacher lecture, the textbook, discrete item and essay tests (both teacher-made and standardized such as the CTBS, the SAT, and the CAP), and challenging subject areas such as social sciences, literature, advanced mathematics, and physical, chemical, and biological sciences. In reality, almost the entire high school and university curriculum can be located in quadrants B and D.

According to research, for second-language speakers CALP takes five or more years to acquire—difficult to accomplish in a four-year high school program. Recall the babble of languages from the visit to Janeane Vigliotti's class? Since English language proficiency lags a bit behind the academic-language proficiency that students have developed in their first languages, they need to use the primary language to help them understand material presented in English.

By facilitating engagement and interaction with academic concepts, sheltered instruction does not "dumb down" the curriculum but rather enriches and contextualizes it. As much as possible, sheltered instruction works by moving the cognitively demanding curriculum from quadrant D (context reduced) to quadrant B (context embedded).

CREATING A SUPPORTIVE ENVIRONMENT IN THE SHELTERED CLASSROOM

Students—Their Characteristics and Their Needs

Students' previous schooling in their first languages and their life experiences as a whole impact on the school's program. Poorly schooled students may labor over such simple tasks as writing their names, forming their letters unevenly, and failing to observe margins and spacing. Even copying from the board may take them what seems like an inordinate amount of time, for, without the ability to take in a group of letters, the untrained eye must remember each letter line-by-line and reproduce it the same way. At the same time, the sheltered classroom may also include students who are highly skilled and completely literate in their primary language. Such students may speak little English but may take Advanced Placement Calculus, for example, or may be unable yet to write complete sentences in English but may be conversant with Hesse's *Steppenwolf* in Korean translation. But for both types of students, without changes of pace or activity, the language they are learning becomes so much "noise" as their ears and brains become fatigued. Variety in the daily agenda helps students remain alert and interested.

The school often assumes that all students have access to books, newspapers, magazines, scissors, glue, colored pencils, and other "tools" found in middle-class homes, and, perhaps more significantly, access to literate family members. But many limited English proficient students live in crowded quarters with no access to a quiet study area. It should not be difficult to imagine what happens to homework when students live with twelve other people in a two-room apartment. Marginal workers, the adults come and go at all hours of the day and night. We have known students who had no place to sleep until an adult had wakened and gone off to work. Even the library may not be an option for a student who must walk there at night through a violence-ridden neighborhood. Indeed, some libraries react to burgeoning student populations by restricting the numbers of those who come to study. In addition, homework may take second place for those engaged in a day-to-day struggle for survival. This is not to argue for no homework, but rather to argue for flexibility and understanding in its assignment.

Teachers generally expect students to be prepared and adequately motivated to engage with the content of the course; students may have a variety of different expectations. Teachers who ask, "Does everyone understand?" often receive a chorus of affirmatives, but test scores may later prove such reassurance to have been premature. Yet, in some cultures, students take all the burden of understanding upon themselves and believe it offensive to tell a teacher, "I don't understand." So great is their respect for teachers that to say, "I don't understand" is tantamount to saying, "You are a poor teacher." Other students, influenced by the competitive climate of the classroom, may not speak for fear of revealing their ignorance or of sounding "funny." One student wrote in his log:

> One thing I am afraid is to speak English, because I am afraid
> the some one or some body would be laughing the way that I
> speak. In my four year of high school that was my problem
> and I never talk out of my head.

The failure of students to "talk out of their heads" not only impedes the free exchange of ideas within the classroom but limits their development as learners.

A *supportive classroom environment* enables the LEP student to succeed in the secondary program. A critical feature of the sheltered classroom is its affective environment. In a climate of trust, students do not fear to speak or to ask questions; the teacher encourages them to risk not-knowing, to dare to inquire, and to see one another as sources of knowledge and information. In sheltered classrooms, empowerment occurs when students find their skills, abilities, and cultures valued and perceived as valuable resources. As students work together, they have opportunities for hands-on and interactive learning, including experiences with collaborative and cooperative learning. Successful sheltered teachers use peer learning to maximum effect when they place students in groups to discuss, share ideas, pool resources, and become one another's supporters. In such groups, as we have seen in Janeane Vigliotti's classroom, it is common for students to use their primary language to assist them in comprehending. This use is not discouraged, for the goals of a lesson always remain comprehension of the concepts as well as production in English. The subtler but equally important lesson taught here is that bilingualism is a valued resource.

The *integration of language skills* also supports LEP students. Listening, speaking, reading, and writing balance and complement one another. Only rarely can students write what they cannot say or read. In sheltered classes, students listen to lessons focused on ideas and concepts, discuss their learning, as well as read and write to integrate new learning with their own personal experiences. Such integration facilitates rapid growth both in the content and in English language proficiency.

As we've mentioned earlier, in a sheltered classroom *contextual clues reinforce content relayed verbally.* The clues include many types of visual aids, including realia and manipulatives such as globes and maps in the social science class; models and specimens in science; and rulers, protractors, and geoboards in mathematics. These multidimensional materials free teachers and students from dependency on only the aural mode of processing, allowing kinesthetic, tactile, and visual ways of learning to help deliver concepts. Graphic organizers (matrices, Venn diagrams, semantic maps and webs) such as we see in Chapter 4 and in the classes we will describe can provide concrete referents for abstract concepts.

In the sections that follow, we will exemplify how teachers and students function in sheltered classrooms—how lessons are planned and delivered, and how students learn. We will begin by describing some ways of creating this supportive environment through the physical arrangement of the classroom, for that physical environment is what envelops us when we pass through its doorway. Then we will show how teachers design lessons that integrate many contextual clues.

Classroom Arrangements to Engage Students

The traditional teacher-centered classroom contains a large desk or table at the front of the classroom and rows of student desks or tables facing it. In this configuration, students are forced to face their teachers and thus interact only with them. Alternative classroom layouts that promote student participation and flexibility in design have much to offer the sheltered classroom. Moving desks, making spaces, and shifting attention from the front of the classroom encourage more student involvement. Students who bashfully or defiantly move to the back of the classroom to sit back and remain uninvolved find it very difficult to do so in a student-centered classroom. Figure 2.2 shows some models of student-centered classrooms. For each model, an example illustrates how flexible the positions of furniture and people can be. It is possible, then, to visualize other arrangements within each of these models to accommodate various sorts of configurations, such as whole-group instruction, large groups, small-group practice, partner practice, and individual work.

As teachers become interested in using their classroom environment as an instructional tool for learning, they begin to reflect on where they place themselves in their classroom. In many student-centered classrooms, the position of the teacher depends on the type of lesson that is being taught. Teryne Dorret remains at the front of her sheltered history class during the opening of class and while she is using the overhead projector to relay information to her students. But when they begin working independently and in groups, she is able to monitor their progress by moving around the room. In addition to assisting with classroom control and keeping students on task, this movement allows Teryne to evaluate her students' progress continuously. Ongoing evaluation is more efficiently done when students are in groups. In one stop, teachers interact with three, four, or five students at a time as opposed to stopping once at every student. By walking around the room and asking questions, teachers can elicit responses from students to find out whether or not students have understood the concepts of the lesson or need further direction.

Movement should not be limited only to the teacher. It is very easy for some students to disengage or tune out when they are forced to remain in their seats throughout their entire school day, particularly if they were used to much greater freedom of movement in the schools of their native countries. Allowing students to get up and move around in a classroom will often engage students who might not otherwise be paying attention. In her advanced English as a second language class, Sandy Okura demonstrates how to sequence a sentence with adjectives and adverbs by taking her students'

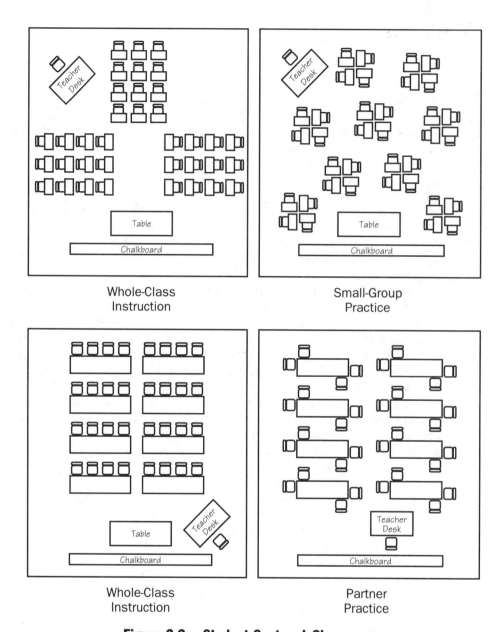

Whole-Class Instruction

Small-Group Practice

Whole-Class Instruction

Partner Practice

Figure 2.2. Student-Centered Classrooms

sentences, writing them on large strips of paper, and cutting out individual words or phrases to make cards.

| The | bright | yellow | sun | disappeared | slowly | behind the mountains |

Individual students are then given the cards; they come up to the front of the room and construct a complete sentence. The students who have adverbs or adverbial phrases discover that they can stand in different locations and the sentence will still make sense. The students become actively involved in the lesson as they get up and position themselves in correct sequential order because the movement keeps them participating. This exercise also encourages students to interact as they help one another decide where to stand.

Contextual Clues to Support Learning

As a visitor walks into Tamara Watson's classroom, it is the large construction paper eye surrounding the clock on the wall that catches the eye. Her transitional ESL students are just finishing a unit entitled "Perspective: The Eye of the Beholder," and the eye serves as a reminder to students of what they are learning. The irony of a clock watching those that watch it is not lost on the students as they go about their daily work. Near "the eye" is a list of vocabulary words that Tamara expects her students to remember from the unit. The words are written on large sheets of butcher paper for all the students to see; the paper shows signs that more words are continually being added. On another wall, a series of prints of flowers illustrate the various perspectives of different artists from Georgia O'Keefe to Vincent Van Gogh. Tamara's classroom is not just a place to house students but a three-dimensional teaching environment.

Many teachers use bulletin boards as backdrops covered in construction paper for posters that they've collected over the years. While these posters may be beautiful, funny, or inspirational, they can be limiting. In most cases, students are never asked to interact with the posters or their messages. Those messages are often culturally bound; sometimes messages like "Thank God It's Friday" suggest negative feelings toward the school. Most importantly, these posters offer no connection to the content or curriculum of the course.

In contrast, Marie Takagaki uses her bulletin boards as another method to convey information about her sheltered math class. Her classes collect math vocabulary instead of posters and cluster the various words around the different math functions they are asked to perform. By the end of the semester, her students have developed a generous vocabulary of words they can use to decipher word problems, formulas, and their math text. More than simply introducing students to individual vocabulary words, the sheltered classroom's bulletin boards can provide students with a context for understanding specific language features unique to the content of the course. The word "boot" might easily be recognized as a shoelike covering for the foot but becomes idiomatic when used in phrases like "paid my rent and my taxes to boot" or "he was booted from the job."

Wall space can be another teaching medium in any classroom, but it is particularly important to sheltered instruction. Displays of student work, maps, charts, timelines, and pictures are all aids to learning. To be truly effective, these displays should be student-produced and directly tied to content. Large sheets of butcher paper taped to the walls provide an excellent and inexpensive surface for students to write language-experience stories, cluster information, or plot graphs. Spread around the classroom, they are easy to read and can be left up as an aid to studying, as Figure 2.3 illustrates.

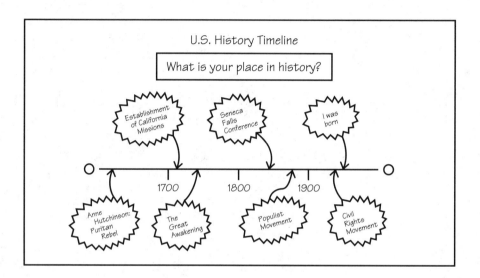

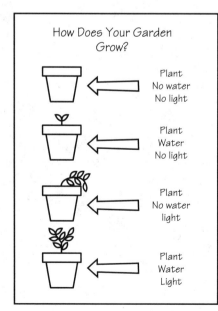

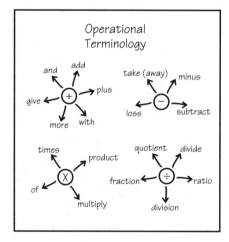

Figure 2.3. Classroom Displays

When available, multimedia equipment enables second-language learners to visualize and hear what they are learning. While such equipment is limited in most situations, "old-fashioned" equipment such as filmstrip projectors can often be found gathering dust in storage rooms. These projectors and other audiovisual aids can be valuable teaching tools. Sheltered social studies teacher Tom Faigin says that he rarely lets a class period go by without using his overhead projector. His beginning students need the additional help of visual association for words like "exploration" as he talks about the Westward Expansion. He helps with this visualization by showing slides or transparencies of pictures of explorers, paintings of the frontier, and maps of the routes taken by explorers.

Frequently, Tom also uses a small tape recorder and a filmstrip projector. He has found if he turns down the sound, he can narrate the filmstrips himself. His narration is more easily understood than the recorded one because the students are more familiar with his voice, he deliberately slows down his reading of the text, and he can gear his vocabulary and syntax to the language acquisition level of his students. He can also stop the narration to elaborate on or clarify key points in the filmstrip. Tom uses a VCR to show movies like *Roots* and *April Morning* because he has found that using literary models to teach history can be very effective. In exploring ways to make the content of an American history class comprehensible, Tom Faigin has become adept at using the many types of media that are available to him.

Lessons Using Contextual Clues and Integrated Language Skills

There are a number of instructional practices to assist language minority students' learning in content area classes. As we noted in discussing Cummins' model earlier in this chapter, using clues that are embedded in context allow students to handle cognitively demanding tasks although they are not yet completely proficient in English. The cluster in Figure 2.4 illustrates the numerous contextual clues available to teachers for use with second-language learners. Many of these contextual clues involve teacher behavior or manipulatives that are brought into the classroom.

One Friday Ron Arreola began his sheltered biology class with a review of the different parts of a flower: the pedicel, receptacle, calyx, pistil, petals, and anthers. Using diagrams and an overhead projector, he had the students label each of the parts on their worksheets and then discuss their functions. But Ron didn't end the lesson with his lecture.

"Now, you are all going to make your own flower," he calmly told them.

"You mean *draw* a flower, don't you?" a student asked.

"No," Ron answered, "I mean *make* a flower."

Students perked up as Ron passed out a paper cup, straws, pieces of wire, marshmallows, and construction paper and demonstrated for the class how to make a flower. In a very short time, each of his students had constructed a flower and with a partner was identifying its parts. At the front of his classroom, Ron

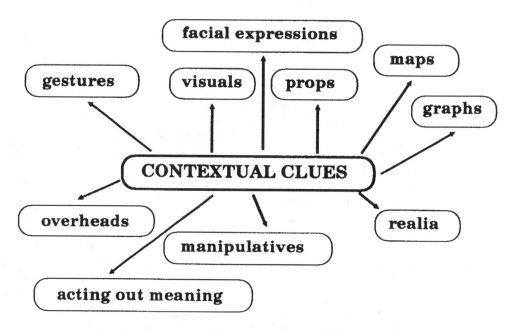

Figure 2.4. Examples of Contextual Clues

wrote a quotation from Georgia O'Keefe on his blackboard: "Still—in a way—nobody sees a flower—really—it is so small—we haven't time, and to see takes time, like to have a friend takes time." Using the quote and their own handmade flower as references, Ron extended the lesson to include additional information about flowers, saying, "It takes time to learn about flowers, to truly see them as Georgia O'Keefe says. So, let's take a look at some and try to identify their distinct characteristics." Using a matrix chart and a large bouquet of different types of flowers, Ron and his students charted out the various structures and functions, as well as the environments in which they live.

In this lesson, Ron Arreola was able to explain to his students that although different types of flowers have the same qualities or parts, they can be very diverse in appearance, environment, and function. By using a variety of instructional practices to teach the structure of a flower, Ron provided his students with enough comprehensible input to allow all of them to understand the concepts. In designing his lesson, he was both creative and flexible, adapting the activities to fit his students.

In a similar way, Marie Takagaki contextualized the concept of probability by bringing pennies into her sheltered math classroom. With partners, students took turns flipping the coins and charting the number of times each penny landed heads or tails. The use of a manipulative as simple as a penny helped students discover the reality, the validity, of understanding how a mathematical concept, such as probability, works. The students' working together in pairs and discussing their results gave them practice in using the language of mathematics.

Ron Rohac had difficulty explaining the concepts of levers or pulleys in his sheltered physical science class, so he brought in a bicycle. With the bicycle

turned upside down, he was able to demonstrate how its le\
constructed and operated. Some students pulled and turr\
bicycle while others described what happened. Using the\
example, Ron was able to bring in other examples of macl\
or pulleys and ask students to apply what they had lear\
these new machines. Pulleys and levers thus become re\
acquiring a new language; having students use the la\
speech or writing reinforces their learning.

Another use of contextual clues to aid second-language learners involves teachers becoming actors, using gestures, facial expressions, and body movement. Picture a literature teacher contextualizing the character of Lenny in *Of Mice and Men* from the flat pages of the text. By shrugging her shoulders, hanging her head, and shuffling through the classroom, the teacher brings Steinbeck's description of Lenny alive for her students. With very little effort, teachers can provide a visual and auditory picture for students and introduce them to the power of the written word. Through acting techniques, they can demonstrate the differences between words like "shuffle," "slide," and "skip" quickly and clearly. Students can chant the words, write them, and demonstrate their meanings themselves.

DESIGNING LESSONS FOR SHELTERED CLASSROOMS

Adapting Language to Learner's Needs

One important way of designing lessons for the sheltered classroom is to keep constantly in mind the need to make the language of the lesson as comprehensible as possible. Several techniques increase comprehensibility:

- Using a slightly slower speech rate
- Enunciating clearly
- Controlling the vocabulary used
- Providing synonyms, antonyms, or other descriptive clues
- Limiting the use of idiomatic expressions
- Allowing pause time for processing new terms
- Using cognates that rename key concepts

All these practices acknowledge the importance of adapting material for students learning English as their second language. Let's listen in on a social science teacher modifying the input of her lesson:

What do we mean when we say "freedom of speech?" What are we free to do? Yes, we are free to speak, free to say what we want. Can you give us some examples of freedom of speech?

Yes, those are excellent examples. You said that we are free to ask questions about our government. We are free to protest against bad situations, things we don't like. We have free speech in the press, the newspapers, and magazines. I like your examples. Can you think of any time when we DON'T have freedom of speech? What restrictions do we place on freedom of speech?

In this short example, the teacher has demonstrated a number of different techniques for modifying input. Her use of the cognates "freedom" and "free" provides students with specific examples of different language forms in use. By repeating, rephrasing, and offering synonyms for essential vocabulary, she has provided additional support for comprehension. Her questions to elicit discussion and examples extend the initial definition of freedom of speech beyond the knowledge or recall stage. It is crucial to reemphasize that making these modifications or adaptions in speaking style and delivery does not constitute "watering down" the curriculum. Instead, it is appreciating the fact that these students are accomplishing two very difficult tasks simultaneously: learning a language and developing expertise in a subject area.

Making Students Active Learners

Dan Fichtner finds that his sheltered social science lessons differ from those for native speakers because his sheltered students need vocabulary development and background knowledge of the concepts he is teaching. He uses a variety of techniques including clustering, mapping, and charting to introduce vocabulary specific to the concepts in history and to encourage students to share what knowledge they have brought with them about the subject. In addition, he always tries to incorporate a variety of activities in all his lessons.

In one lesson, he wanted to introduce his students to the California Gold Rush. He identified the key concepts he wanted his students to learn: the psychology of the pioneer, the growth of the cities, and the "get rich quick" mentality. Because he recognized his students' lack of experience with the concepts, he began by reading Mark Twain's "Jumping Frog of Calaveras County" out loud to his students and playing music that reflected the flavor of the time. His students then read maps that identified the three main routes to the gold fields, discussed the types of shops that would be needed in a boom town, and picked out and practiced vocabulary from the text in cooperative learning groups. As follow-up activities, Dan's students created a boomtown newspaper, wrote a diary entry from the perspective of a pioneer child, and role-played dialogues between customers and owners using store front pieces they had made. Throughout his lesson, Dan provided his students with a venue for acquiring language through the concepts they were learning as they st⌐ history of the Gold Rush.

Janeane Vigliotti has discovered that she must create a number of mater⌐ for her lessons herself. She has brought art materials, rulers, magazines, and newspapers into her history and geography classes; students use them to make their own maps, visual aids, and class projects. She also plans her lessons to include many references to the backgrounds of the students she is working with in each class; as she says, "Language acquisition is more meaningful when related to culture and the primary language." Janeane explains that the challenges of devising lessons for second-language learners "bring out the skill of being a teacher."

CONCLUDING REMARKS

In this chapter we have attempted to portray the sheltered classroom by depicting teachers at work. Recall that ideal students for the sheltered classroom are those of intermediate fluency. These students have acquired the receptive and productive skills that allow them to negotiate both spoken and contextual meanings in English. Such students have had successful ESL experiences and have developed English literacy. Unfortunately, as we visited schools and talked with other teachers, we found multiple instances of students with lower levels of proficiency in sheltered classrooms. They and their teachers were struggling.

Despite a critical shortage of qualified bilingual teachers, students whose English proficiency is newly emerging should properly be placed in content courses taught in their primary languages. But in order to give students a full program, beginning students of English are often inappropriately placed in sheltered content courses although they are not yet linguistically prepared. The resulting failure cannot be attributed to lack of academic preparation or motivation but primarily to their level of English proficiency. In our classroom portraits, we focused on successful strategies with students of intermediate fluency in English.

In constructing these vignettes, we interviewed many teachers. Our conversations with successful sheltered content teachers revealed a diversity of backgrounds: they were former elementary bilingual teachers, high school teachers, and college teachers from a multitude of disciplines. All were united in their dedication to making content comprehensible. Few set out to become "sheltered" teachers, but evolved as instructional specialists when they were arbitrarily assigned to a subject area class containing only limited-English-speaking students. Undaunted, our teacher subjects responded with interest and enthusiasm to the challenge of becoming sheltered teachers.

These experienced sheltered content teachers characterize themselves as "flexible" and "creative" and speak consistently of devising lessons and materials for the purpose of focusing a concept for their audience. Visitors to their classrooms are impressed by the hum of productivity: students confer in many languages, point to illustrations or maps, handle specimens and lab equipment,

- Develop a student-centered environment
- Arrange tables or desks to allow for varied group configurations
- Use wall space as a teaching surface (bulletin boards, student work display, butcher paper writing assignments, student-made charts or graphs)
- Remain in continuous contact with students by walking around the room and observing student work and behavior
- Provide varied opportunities for students to interact, ask questions, and practice (in front of the class, student to teacher alone, student to student, in groups)
- Use visual and audiovisual equipment as permanent fixtures in the classroom
- Use contextual clues like models and pictures to help with comprehension
- Include hands-on, vocabulary, cooperative, and group activities
- Modify your language to increase comprehensibility and check frequently for understanding
- Plan topically focused lessons that actively involve the student by including listening and speaking activities that reinforce reading and writing activities

Figure 2.5. Guidelines for Teaching a Sheltered Content Class

and use their texts as references for answering questions. These teachers are constantly in motion, pointing, sketching, gesturing, conferring with students, sitting in with groups, listening carefully to a question, and calling the whole class to focus on the answer.

These teachers continue to seek out and receive training in their academic fields. All reported attending staff development sessions in their districts; some have participated in county training sessions for ESL methodology and cooperative learning; others have enrolled in graduate courses at local universities. All mentioned professional conferences as a source of inspiration and learning. But most importantly, when we asked sheltered teachers to characterize their own growth process, they spoke of "learning about learning," feeling energized by the skills demanded of them, and of becoming better teachers as they empowered their students with knowledge of concepts and confidence in their developing English language skills.

ASSISTANCE

California Association for Bilingual Education (CABE)
926 J Street, Suite 810
Sacramento, CA 95814

California Teachers of English to Speakers of Other Languages
(CATESOL)
P.O. Box 4082
Whittier, CA 90607

Center for Academic Interinstitutional Programs (CAIP)
UCLA
Gayley Center, Suite 304
405 Hilgard Avenue
Los Angeles, CA 90024

ERIC/CLL
ERIC Clearinghouse on Languages and Linguistics
Center for Applied Linguistics
1118 22nd Street, NW
Washington, DC 20037

IRA
International Reading Association
800 Barksdale Road
Newark, DE 19714

NCTE
National Council of Teachers of English
1111 West Kenyon Road
Urbana, IL 61801-1096

TESOL
Teachers of English to Speakers of Other Languages
1600 Cameron Street, Suite 300
Alexandria, VA 22314

FOR FURTHER READING

Crandall, J., Dale, T. C., Cuevas, G. J., Kessler, C., Quinn, M. E., King, M., Fagan, B., Bratt, T., and Baer, R. (1987). *ESL through content-area instruction: Mathematics, science, social studies.* Englewood Cliffs, NJ: Prentice Hall Regents.
  Thorough analysis of content areas and the specific language-related difficulties they pose for the LEP student. Integrates linguistic, cognitive, and second-language acquisition theories. Specificity makes this a valuable resource.

Crandall, J., Dale, T. C., Rhodes, N. C., and Spanos, G. (1987). *English skills for algebra. Math-language activities for algebra students* [student text]. Englewood Cliffs, NJ: Prentice Hall Regents.
  Mathematics/language approach that integrates learning of English language skills with acquisition of basic concepts in algebra. Language is the vehicle for thinking about and discussing the processes used to perform basic operations in algebra. Particularly useful for understanding textbook language.

Cummins, J. (1981). The role of primary language development in promoting educational success for language minority students. In California Office of Bilingual Bicultural Education. In *Schooling and language minority students: A theoretical framework.* Sacramento, CA: California State Department of Education.
  Seminal article for all educators. Clarifies the role of primary language and its relationship to academic and cognitive development. Suggests a common underlying proficiency between first and second language.

Cummins, J. (1989). *Empowering minority students.* Sacramento, CA: California Association for Bilingual Education.
  Focus on linguistic discrimination and the school failure of language minority children. Argues powerfully for empowerment and enablement through critical literacy, cooperative learning, and process writing.

Fathman, A. K., Quinn, M. E. (1989). *Science for language learners* [student text]. Englewood Cliffs, NJ: Prentice Hall Regents.

Five units focused on the theme of energy: encourages critical thinking skills, vocabulary development. Many good ideas for incorporating graphics, small group discussion, and integrating reading and writing skills with science.

Heimlich, J. E., Pittelman, S. D. (1986). *Semantic mapping: Classroom applications.* Newark, DE: International Reading Association.

Contains practical applications of several types of semantic maps drawn from elementary and middle school classes in several content areas. Well-developed explanation of the role of graphic organizers in vocabulary development, prewriting exercises, and reading comprehension.

Levine, M. G. (1990). Sheltering U.S. history for limited English proficient students. *Social Studies Review*, 30 (Fall): 27–39.

Suggests four reading/writing activities for sheltered U.S. History course. All are developed with reference to Cummins's quadrant; Levine locates them as quadrant B—context embedded and cognitively demanding.

Northcutt, L., Watson, D. (1986). *S.E.T. Sheltered English teaching handbook.* San Marcos, CA: AM Graphics and Printing.

Defines sheltered English as a step-by-step process that makes content meaningful. Pragmatic advice useful for teachers of multilevel classrooms. Focus on planning sheltered English lessons.

Schifini, A. (1985). *Sheltered English: Content area instruction for limited English proficient students.* Los Angeles, CA: Los Angeles County Office of Education.

Defines sheltered English as strategies for making input comprehensible. Explanation of instructional strategies underlying the approach and discussion of the four English language skill areas. Useful appendices.

Sutman, F. X., Allen, V. F., and Shoemaker, F. (1986). *Learning English through science: A guide to collaboration for science teachers. English teachers, and teachers of English as a second language.* Washington, DC: National Science Teachers Association.

Sheltered English from the perspective of science teachers. Describes lessons at the university, community college, and kindergarten levels. Contains several model lessons.

Writing and Language Socialization across Cultures: Some Implications for the Classroom

George Gadda

All of us recognize differences between languages—we know that the sounds of Spanish differ from those of Chinese. If we've studied a language other than English, we're probably also aware that languages differ from each other in the ways they form words and combine words to create sentences. We know that students' first languages can influence their English, and that the pronunciations or constructions likely to prove difficult for speakers of one language will differ from those difficult for speakers of other languages. Language teachers know how to predict these differences, and all of us are aware of them to some extent.

What may be much less clear to us is that languages also differ in their rhetorics—that is, in the way they use language to accomplish various purposes, particularly in writing. Along with the structural elements of language—sounds, words, syntax—we all learn rules about what can and should be said, and how, and when. Some of this rhetoric is formally taught in school; some of it we internalize in less direct ways, simply by observing what is typical and esteemed in our culture. Since few native speakers of English have the advanced literacy required to be nativelike writers in a second language, very few of us have had the experience of conceptualizing the way things are most usually and effectively said or written in a language not our own. Differences in rhetoric may be opaque for us, and as unexpected to others as my own surprised realization in first-year French that place names change from language to language.

This chapter has three parts. First it considers some of the differences among written texts identified by the study of contrastive rhetoric. Then, drawing on the work of Shirley Brice Heath, it addresses the related question of how children are socialized to use language and how that socialization may or may not aid them in the kind of analytical thinking and writing typical of higher education in the West. Finally, the chapter suggests some uses that we as teachers can make of the insights derived from the work of contrastive rhetoricians and ethnographers of language, including a rationale for the approaches to teaching offered in Chapters 2, 4, and 5.

CONTRASTIVE RHETORIC

Since 1966 scholars in a discipline called contrastive rhetoric have examined the writing produced in English by writers schooled in other countries to determine the ways in which their texts differ from those produced by native speakers of English. Although all of their work is exploratory rather than definitive, it does give us as teachers insight into some ways in which nonnative speakers' writing in English may not meet the English-speaking reader's expectations.

The still-significant first study, Robert Kaplan's "Cultural Thought Patterns in Intercultural Education," was in fact motivated by the desire to explain why papers by foreign students often generated from instructors comments like, "The material is all here, but it seems somehow out of focus" (Kaplan, 1966, p. 3). Kaplan analyzed hundreds of expository compositions written in English by students whose first languages included Arabic, Chinese, Korean, and Spanish to determine how their paragraphs were organized.[1] He concluded that there were predictable differences between paragraphs written in English by students with various first languages; to describe these differences Kaplan wrote that "superficially, the movement of the various paragraphs . . . may be graphically represented in the following manner:

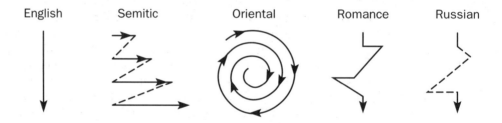

English   Semitic   Oriental   Romance   Russian

Kaplan cautions, however, that "Much more detailed and more accurate descriptions are required before any meaningful contrastive system can be elaborated" (p. 15).

Based on the available evidence, however, Kaplan observes that in Arabic "paragraph development is based on a complex series of parallel constructions, both positive and negative. This kind of parallelism may most clearly be demonstrated in English by reference to the King James version of the Old Testament." Of Chinese and Korean compositions, he observes that

> Some Oriental writing, on the other hand, is marked by what may be called an approach by indirection. . . . [It shows the subject] from a variety of tangential views, but the subject is never looked at directly. Things are developed in terms of what they are not, rather than in terms of what they are. Again, such a development in a modern English paragraph would strike the English reader as awkward and unnecessarily indirect. (p. 10)

Kaplan contrasts both of these models of development with the "linear" coherence of the textbook English expository paragraph, whether it is structured inductively (specifics leading to a generalization) or deductively (generalization followed by supporting details).[2]

Subsequently there have been a number of studies of the texts produced in English by writers schooled in other languages and rhetorical traditions. Among the topics such studies have examined are paragraph structures, means of highlighting topics, and ways of establishing coherence between sentences and paragraphs. Some studies have also considered the differences between whole texts produced by native English speakers and nonnatives in response to the same stimulus. Two interesting studies have compared stories written by native speakers with stories written to the same topic by nonnatives.

One of these studies compared the narratives written by 223 students in a group of eight Australian schools in 1984. The students were sixth- and eleventh-grade native speakers of Arabic, Vietnamese, and English; the writing they produced was "a bedtime story to a child younger than the writer" written in a forty-minute class period (Söter, 1988, p. 181). The researcher, Anna O. Söter, found that all three language groups produced stories with setting, character, and action, though the elements were used in different proportions. The native speakers of English approximated the conventions of conventional bedtime stories most closely, with their focus on the plot of the story conveying "a strong sense of forward movement" (p. 195). In contrast, the Vietnamese students placed less emphasis on plot, more on the relationship between characters and their inner states. Their concern with character manifested itself in a much greater proportion of dialogue in their stories than in those of the other two groups; Söter reports that Vietnamese informants identify these traits as typical of Vietnamese narratives in general. The Arabic speakers were also influenced by the style of narratives in their first language, Söter suggests; in comparison with the other two groups, the Arabic writers devoted considerably more attention to setting than did the native English speakers or the Vietnamese. She also notes that some of the narratives by Arabic speakers in the eleventh grade would not be culturally appropriate as bedtime stories in the West.

A similar study by Chantanee Indrasuta (1988) compares stories or narrative compositions written in English by thirty U.S. high school seniors with those by thirty Thai high school seniors in both Thai and English. Indrasuta found that the American and Thai compositions written to the topics "I Made a Hard Decision" and "I Succeeded, At Last" were similar in the kinds of cohesive ties they used, in their reliance on chronological organization, and in the proportions of description, dialogue, and generalization they included.

But there were also significant differences, differences often explained by interviews with the writers and their teachers. Though both American and Thai teachers and students agreed that the purpose of narrative is "to inform and to entertain," the Thai writers, perhaps influenced by the Buddhist tradition, conceived of narrative as intended to instruct, to point to a stated moral. Thai writers also thought their stories had to be true; if they had no real experience that fit the specifications of the title, they didn't create one. Finally, Thai students used considerably more figurative language than Americans, perhaps "because analogy appears to be the preferred way of describing things in Thai" (p. 219). In contrast, American students understood the primary purpose of narrative to be capturing their audience's interest. Because they believed their primary task was to entertain the reader, they felt able to create a story or to reconceive a true one "to create surprise and suspense" (p. 221). The language of the American compositions was considerably less formal than that of the Thai compositions—much less likely to use figurative language, and much more likely to approximate colloquial speech. In all, Indrasuta suggests that the Thai and American students were reproducing two different cultural models of narrative, even when they were responding to the same writing assignment.

HOW CHILDREN ARE SOCIALIZED TO USE LANGUAGE: WAYS WITH WORDS

Such differences in ideas about language use can exist between subcultures as well as between cultures. The most comprehensive study of such differences is Shirley Brice Heath's *Ways with Words*, the result of ten years of ethnographic work the author did in the Piedmont section of the Carolinas in the 1960s. This was a period of transition in Carolina schools similar to the flux currently being experienced in California schools; in the Carolinas, however, the students newly entering the schools were not emigrants from many nations, as in California today, but the black children who had been excluded from the white school system before the Supreme Court struck down "separate but equal" schooling in 1954's *Brown v. Board of Education*. A linguist and anthropologist, Heath was at the time working in teacher-training and in-service programs.

When elementary and high schools were desegregated in the Piedmont area of the Carolinas in the late 1960s, middle-class teachers were suddenly faced with classes that included black children whose ways of using language—not just or even primarily the forms of that language—made it difficult for them to meet their teachers' expectations for performance in class, or even to understand what these were. The teachers' classes had always included the children of white mill workers, whose performance did not match that of children from mainstream "townspeople" families. However, the addition of a group of children whose socialization was apparently so different from that of the other two groups made the need for background information crucial to the teachers.

As a result, for the next several years Heath frequently visited a community of working-class, white mill workers she calls "Roadville" and a working class black community she calls "Trackton." Out of her long-term observation of both communities, Heath draws portraits of the radically different ways in which children learned to use language in them. When compared with a similar portrait of the way children were socialized to use language in what she called "Townspeople" families, both black and white, this information allowed teachers to reconsider their own ways of using language in the classroom and to clarify and define their own expectations about how students will perform there.

From the beginning, children in Roadville were engaged in dialogues by their parents and other adults, who used those dialogues to teach children how to do things "right." When naming things and displaying other knowledge, including knowledge about behavioral rules and moral judgments, Roadville children were always expected to produce a particular expected answer, even if other answers were accurate given the stimulus. Just as the fundamentalist Protestantism in which they were raised relied on the exact recall and literal interpretation of the Bible, so did everything else in the Roadville children's linguistic environment encourage the assumption that there was a single right answer to every question.

The experience of black children in Trackton was very different. Adults in Trackton did not modify their speech to children, and seldom did they engage them in dialogues. When they did, the purpose of those dialogues was never to have children display knowledge that adults already possessed. Especially if they were male, children were expected to find ways to assert themselves and to perform on the stage formed metaphorically by the open area at the center of the community and the porches that bordered it. In its oral communication, the community valued word play, imaginative and often fictionalized retellings of actual incidents, and, in general, the adroit use of language to mediate shifting moods and power relationships in Trackton itself. Children in Trackton were not always held to literal accuracy and were not usually asked to hypothesize. They were not encouraged to think of themselves as addressing audiences outside Trackton itself.

From the time their children were very small, Townspeople of both races modified their speech to make it comprehensible to children and engaged them in dialogues whose purpose was usually to teach the children or to assess what they knew. From an early age, parents read books with children; these encounters were filled with questions in which children were asked to provide information about the text or the pictures ("What's in front of the house?") or to form hypotheses about it ("What will happen next?"). In all, children were encouraged to use language in ways that fostered a view of themselves as able to report information, to manipulate it to form hypotheses and inter-pretations, and to assume a role in public discourse in which these activities would be pursued among people who were not members of the child's immediate community.

These differing backgrounds had given the three groups of children understandings of what counts as a "story" as different as those of the Arabic, Vietnamese, Thai, and native English speakers described above. For children in Trackton, a story was a narrative calculated to show off their creativity as storytellers. While often based in fact, the story didn't need to be; it would be esteemed by the Trackton audience to the extent that it was clever (for example, by paraphrasing a familiar story or by commenting obliquely on a relationship in the community) and verbally inventive (for example, by playing with proverbs or with quotations from songs, television shows, or other parts of popular culture). Everything in their preschool environment led Trackton children to think that to "tell a story" was to make one up and to embellish and perform it engagingly. These expectations contrasted sharply with those of Roadville.

Among Roadville families, a "story" was a strictly true report of an actual incident told to illustrate a moral based on the model of often retold stories from the Bible. Such stories were told only by members of the community who were agreed to be skilled storytellers, and they had as their purpose reconfirming the moral and underlining human frailty. In ways predictable from Roadville's fundamentalist Protestantism, fictionalizing actual experience in any particular was considered to be a "lie." Among the Townspeople, in contrast, a "story" could be a factual account, but was more usually a fictional story introduced by a formula like "Once upon a time"—a story whose purpose was neither to instruct in Roadville's terms nor to entertain in the particular ways valued in Trackton. Clearly, the request to "tell a story" will produce in children from these three communities quite different sets of expectations; equally clear is the fact that the understanding most in line with the school's expectations is the one controlled by the children of the Townspeople. As a result, they were most likely to respond to assignments in ways that their teachers would value.

The differences between the ways in which these three groups of children had been socialized to use language had important influences on their chances for success in school in other ways as well. The kinds of questioning to which they'd been exposed were particularly important. Children from Trackton were completely unaccustomed to—even bewildered by—the kinds of questions they were asked from the beginning of their formal schooling: questions that asked them to name objects, describe their properties—in many ways to display knowledge they knew the teacher already had. Children from Roadville did well with these questions in grades 1 through 3 but began to fall behind as the curricular emphasis in grades 4 and 5 shifted from display of memorized knowledge to its application in new situations (Heath, 1982, p. 64). The children who did best in meeting the demands of the school's curriculum as it became steadily more demanding conceptually were those of the mainstream families. It might be said that all of their socialization in language had given them a view of themselves as purposeful communicators—people who could observe, discuss what they observed, evaluate, and solve problems with language—the view that the high school curriculum also presupposed.

Heath undertook her ethnographic research as a way of helping teachers change their teaching in ways that would offer a greater chance of success to children whose previous experiences with language in their homes and communities were different from those the school assumed and would draw upon. Once they had this information, teachers could begin to make the expectations of their classrooms clearer to children whose previous experience had not already accustomed them to its patterns. Based on her own observations and on other research, Heath identifies several uses of language as both central to success in school and practiced in the mainstream home:

- Labeling parts of the environment
- Discussing their features
- Considering their uses and origins
- Hypothesizing alternatives about them

The challenge for teachers is to help students who don't already control these uses of language to add them to the repertoire these students bring to school.

Approaching the question of educational success from a different perspective—the perspective of what college and university writing assignments require—in 1988, William Walsh and I identified a parallel list of abilities. To perform well on writing assignments designed to elicit analysis—writing intended to define and explain the significance of subject matter—we concluded that students needed these abilities:

- Reading closely for important details and for organizing patterns, including those hitherto unrecognized or thought insignificant
- Selecting and organizing those details and patterns
- Drawing defensible inferences and generalizations from what is read or observed
- Evaluating and reevaluating the usefulness of those inferences and generalizations, testing them against competing ideas and the data (Gadda and Walsh, 1988, p. 20)

In describing the purposes of college and university writing assignments, we quote ESL researcher Daniel Horowitz's conclusion that "most professors who have been trained in English-language universities place a high value on reintegration of data and that many writing tasks are, in fact, expressly designed to provide opportunities of demonstrating this ability" (1986, p. 458).

Thus, we support Horowitz's view that, to help language minority students succeed in higher education, we must do more than teach them the forms and structures of English. We must also help them understand how English is used for academic purposes in our schools and what kinds of discourse we value. As much as possible, we must help our students become comfortable with those ways of using language and claim them as their own.

LANGUAGE SOCIALIZATION AND LANGUAGE MINORITY STUDENTS

How do these insights gained from native speakers affect our work with language minority students? What has been observed about the ways in which language minority students are socialized to use language and the ways in which that socialization matches the expectations of our schools?

There has been no language socialization study of any group of language minority students as encompassing as *Ways with Words*. In the volume *Beyond Language,* however, Shirley Brice Heath reports on work undertaken in the last ten years by graduate-student ethnographers at the University of California at Berkeley and at Stanford University. We will focus here on what they have observed about language socialization among Chinese families and among working-class families that have recently emigrated from rural Mexico.[3] These groups are of particular interest given the number of students from these backgrounds that California's schools will serve into the foreseeable future.

Working-Class Mexican Families Recently Arrived from Mexico

The researchers whose work Heath reports describe the language socialization of children in working-class families recently emigrated from rural Mexico. The thrust of this socialization focused on training children to fulfill their expected roles in the family. Parents and elders are figures of authority; children are expected to be polite and respectful to their elders, and it is this aspect of language use on which parents focus their attention and their teaching. Adults and children form separate conversational groups on social occasions; children listen to elders, obey them, and answer questions they are asked, but they do not ask adults questions or begin conversations with them themselves. Often adults tease children, commenting playfully on the child's distinctive characteristics, relationship to the teaser, or suggesting a cruel but obviously fictional action. As the child responds, the exchange underlines and reinforces the familial or social relationship between the two. Much parental teaching proceeds by modeling rather than by verbal instruction: parents show children what to do and correct them as they imitate rather than explaining a whole process or asking questions designed to lead the child to the next step. (Middle-class Mexican mothers use the latter strategies, however; in a 1984 study of Mexican mothers of various socioeconomic backgrounds teaching their children new tasks, Laosa [1977] found that Mexican mothers with high school educations more frequently used the questioning method typical of similarly educated Anglos.)

We have already seen the significance of the kinds of questions parents typically ask their children for the children's easy acculturation to the school. The kinds of questioning ethnographers have observed as typical of the working-class Mexican home differ from those of Roadville, Trackton, and the Townspeople. Heath reports that recently emigrated working-class Mexican parents "seldom ask questions that require children to repeat facts, rehearse the sequence of events, or foretell what they will do" (1986, p. 161). When children are asked to name things, Heath notes, it is usually in the context of large social gatherings, not day-to-day family interactions, and the items labeled are likely to be people's names, parts of the body, or ongoing activities. In other words, the questioning activity once again serves a primary purpose of reinforcing relationships within the family and its immediate social situation. Questions seldom focus on information derived from outside the family circle—for example, from media or public life—and parents do not usually ask questions about information they already possess. They may ask questions aimed at learning about behavior in contexts they don't know: "Were you good in school today?" Again, the emphasis of the language exchange on appropriate behavior seems clear.

Working-class families recently arrived from rural Mexico may not have children's books at home; Heath notes that story books are available in Mexican schools, but that publishers in Mexico do not promote books for children in the way that publishers in the United States and Europe do. (Heath emphasizes that lack of children's books in the home is thus not a sign that families are not concerned about supporting children's readiness for school.) Whether or not they have books, children from these families do have experience with storytelling; Heath notes that "stories fill many hours in Mexican-American homes; young and old tell scary *bruja* (witch) tales, as well as stories about real events embellished with new details and about historical figures and events" (p. 174). But these stories may not match the American school's definition of story, and the American school's emphasis on individual work conflicts with a much stronger group orientation in Mexican education.

Chinese Families

Like working-class Mexican families, Chinese families socialize children to use language in ways that reinforce a social system. In this case, the social system is one that Heath characterizes as valuing "age, authority, perfection, restraint, and practical achievements" and as focusing on the importance of social roles determined by sex and age rather than individual characteristics or preferences (p. 158). Describing the general plan for raising children, Heath says:

> Parents see themselves as primary agents in directing children to assume in appropriate fashion the roles that the community expects of boys and girls, and later young men and women. Children must defer to adults, who determine what their children can do and tell them when they should do it. Children are encouraged to model themselves after authorities, to listen to authorities and watch what they do, and finally to practice again and again to achieve perfection. Learning is centered on the situation rather than the individual. (1986, p. 158)

While socialization in the working-class Mexican family focuses on producing a dutiful and respectful child with close affectional ties to others in the immediate environment, the Chinese process places primary emphasis on excellence in fulfilling a role prescribed by a larger social system.

Specifically in terms of language socialization, this respect for the role of authority means that parents control verbal interactions with their children. They choose topics for discussion and direct the flow of conversation; they pay attention to what their children say and correct them when necessary, treating language like any other kind of behavior. Unlike working-class Mexican parents, Chinese parents ask children factual questions and talk about the steps they are following as they perform a task. Mothers, in particular, may read to young children and lead them in art projects or other educational activities. It could be said, then, that Chinese parents see themselves as active teachers of language.

We have seen the importance of questioning in relation to other groups and the expectations of schooling. Chinese parents have been observed to ask questions about fact, requesting names of things in the environment or the appropriateness of various behaviors for people of a certain age or sex. Chinese parents also ask children to describe processes, activities, and books. Heath notes, however, that these questions are likely to mirror the general preference for reinforcing the behavior appropriate to social roles rather than individual emotion:

> [Questions] from parents to children do not usually include expressions of emotional evaluations. . . . Adults' comments about books or acquaintances do not model . . . interpretations based on emotions; for example, parents are not likely to say of a storybook character who has lost his way in the forest, "He's probably very sad and wishing he were home with his mother right now." They are much more likely to say, "He's lost in the forest. How could that happen to a little boy?" (1986, p. 172).

The questions Chinese parents ask thus prepare their children for many of the school's demands, but not necessarily for the Western school's openness to individual interpretation.

What is the result of this language socialization? In a 1989 article Fan Shen, who grew up in China and is now a graduate student in English at Marquette University, discusses his need to value individual perception much more highly in the U.S. educational system. Responding to Chinese culture's respect for authority, he recalls once in China "willfully attributing some of my own thoughts to 'experts' when I needed some arguments but could not find a suitable quotation from a literary or political 'giant' " (Shen, 1989, p. 460). In the United States, on the other hand, his task in writing has been to construct a *persona* that is sufficiently confident and assertive, though "immodest" in Chinese terms. Confirming Kaplan's observations, he also comments on his need to learn a new way of thinking about the sequence of ideas in writing.

In her autobiography *Fifth Chinese Daughter,* Jade Snow Wong suggests some similar discontinuities between her home culture and that of U.S. academics. Wong, who grew up in a Chinese family in San Francisco during the 1930s and 1940s, recalls her bewilderment in her first college class using the Socratic method:

> What was disturbing in the first weeks at Mills [College] was that her lifelong perfected system of learning failed her. At the end of several weeks, she had only a handful of lecture notes. The instructor of the labor course, a brilliant and direct man as interested in the practical workings of theory as in the theory itself, taught by encouraging questions. But at the end of every never-dull class period, Jade Snow did not have one lecture note.
>
> How was she going to study without notes? Accustomed to specific assignments in orderly fashion, and habitually

thorough, she became concerned by the vagueness of subjects which defeated her ability to memorize—an carefully perfected by her Chinese studies and whic heretofore always worked.

Impressed by the informality and approachability professors, she gathered her courage to speak to he instructor. "I have a problem in not being able to take any lecture notes from you. At junior college, we were given definite outlines to follow and study for examinations."

Her instructor seemed amused. "Why do you think that you learn only from lecture notes?"

Jade Snow had no answer to this unexpected question.

He continued, "Here we want to know each one individually. Instead of reading a set of prepared notes, I study my students' minds and ideas. By the conversational method, I try to develop your minds, not give you sets of facts. Don't you know that you can always go to the library to look up facts?"

Jade Snow could not immediately grasp this new concept of individual training. She had never thought of the purpose of academic training as being anything else than that of disseminating superior information. (Wong, 1945, pp. 161–62).

Wong's language experience at home, and even in American schools, had not given her the concept of analysis as we've defined it here.

WHAT CAN WE AS TEACHERS DO?

Everything in this chapter so far must be understood as reporting some cultural differences in discourse and language socialization as they are currently understood. One thing we must *never* do is assume that these descriptions define the experience or characteristics of any particular student. Researchers typically report as large a range of difference between members of a group as between groups; the fact that Jade Snow Wong and Fan Shen report having internalized authoritarian ideas about schooling does not suggest that any individual Chinese student will share their experience. In other words, we must avoid stereotyping.

Another thing we can't do is to restructure our classrooms or our curricular expectations to match what we suspect our students' backgrounds may be. Such changes would not be possible even if all our students came from one ethnic or national group, one socioeconomic class, and one educational background— as of course they don't. The individual differences already referred to would also render such a plan useless, not to mention the needs and expectations of the society for which we prepare students.

What we can do is find teaching strategies that help students of all language socializations and discourse experiences participate in the school's culture of literacy. It's worth reflecting that the culture of the school is not the home culture of *any* student. Though the alignment between the cultures of the school and that of homes like those of Heath's Townspeople may be relatively close, any experienced teacher of writing to college-age native speakers from Townspeople homes knows that they don't achieve profiency in what this chapter calls analytical writing without explanation, instruction, and conscious practice. The suggestions for teaching that follow are not for nonnative speakers of English only; they are useful and effective with all groups of students. But these strategies are particularly useful for students whose home cultures are at some distance from our schools' expectations about language use for academic purposes.

As Heath notes, "The school can promote academic and vocational success for all children, regardless of their first-language background, by providing the *greatest possible range of oral and written language use*" (1986, p. 144). Encouraging students to write and talk about mathematics or history in a broad range of ways will support both their mastery of language itself and their comprehension and retention of subject matter. Where possible, Heath suggests adapting forms of speech already used in the community to academic purposes (rap songs to teach biology, for example), as well as providing instruction and guided practice in forms of speaking and writing with which students may not already be familiar. Collaborative learning techniques can allow students who are relatively skilled in these language uses to help those who aren't. A wide range of language uses for sheltered classrooms can be found in Chapter 2 and many suggestions for writing-to-learn in Chapter 5.

Discussing with students *models of the kinds of writing they must produce* is a useful instructional practice with all populations. If students have never studied effective persuasive essays or lab reports, the likelihood that they'll write them successfully is small. Useful for all students, modeling is particularly important for students whose internalized sense of the way written texts work may differ from those of the English-speaking reader. In demonstrating analytical writing, it may be particularly useful to focus attention on these features:

- How the writer introduces the subject or issue
- How the writer states his or her own position or thesis
- How the writer incorporates or acknowledges the writing of others
- How the text achieves coherence, both through linked ideas and through text features like transitions

One caution: it's usually best to provide at least two good models of any one kind of writing. Contrasting the two pieces can help students see the range of possibilities within the form as well as what's essential to it.

Fostering a critical attitude toward written texts may be particularly useful for students whose home cultures regard texts as uniquely authoritative *because* they are written. Many cultures do not share the Western habit of regarding texts as invitations to interpretation and response. Carolyn Matalene notes that in

China her students would tell her, "We have *learned* the story," and they would in fact have memorized it. The usual Chinese response to a literary text is to repeat it, not to paraphrase, analyze, or interpret it" (1985, p. 791). Students who deal with texts in this way will benefit from activities that cause them to manipulate texts, to articulate their own ideas about the issues the texts raise, and to see themselves as interpreters. Besides supporting their acquisition of written language, the activities presented in Chapter 4 to exemplify the "into, through, and beyond" model will help students become comfortable with the attitudes toward texts that Western academic analysis requires. Teachers can also model the process of reading a text actively, questioning its premises and the reasons for its stylistic choices. A similar questioning attitude toward their own texts and those of their peers lies behind the commenting models provided in Chapter 5.

Explaining Western ideas about using others' texts in one's own writing can be particularly important for students whose cultures employ allusion to well-known texts as an esteemed feature of style. Matalene (1985) notes that:

> It is, any literate Chinese will insist, "an absolute fact" that to be a good writer requires wide reading in the Chinese classics. Only through such readings in classical Chinese can a writer become equipped with the phrases, sayings, and literary allusions necessary to "ornament and enliven" discourse. . . . (p. 793)

Such quotations are not identified as such; neither are quotations from the Koran which Arabic-speaking students may incorporate in their writing. While it's true that Western writers can incorporate or allude to extremely well-known quotations from the Bible or from Shakespeare without quotation marks or documentation, in writing for school and most other public purposes we assume that words, syntax, and ideas are those of the writer unless we're explicitly told otherwise. This expectation of Western readers may need to be made equally explicit to writers from other cultures. Of course, helping students acquire academic conventions of using and citing texts is a major concern of those who teach writing to native speakers as well.

Finally, *using students as informants about their own language use* can help teachers understand how to help their students meet the English-speaking reader's expectations more effectively. We have seen how different cultural and subcultural groups have different ideas of what a story is; clearly, it's impossible for us as teachers to know all the ideas about various forms of discourse our individual students bring with them to the classroom. But we can ask them. If the texts our students produce seem to violate our expectations in systematic ways, we can ask them why —individually, or, if the puzzling traits are common, as a class. Here are some questions we might pose:

- Why did you begin and end the piece this way?
- How do you think this kind of writing should sound?

- What do you think your readers already know about what you say?
- What do you think you have to tell them?
- How do you expect your readers to follow you from point 1 to point 2?
- What do you expect your readers to understand by this?
- How do you expect this piece of writing to affect your readers?

By asking students to tell us how they arrived at texts that we find puzzling, we may be able to learn what conceptions they have that conflict with ours. And doing that may help us to see ourselves with different eyes as well.

NOTES

1. This article named contrastive rhetoric and initiated its study. Kaplan's method in it has been questioned; in particular, it has been asked whether the "cultural thought patterns" referred to in the title can be reliably gauged from writing produced in English, and whether these are as deterministic as Kaplan's references to the Sapir/Whorf hypothesis might seem to claim. Whatever these reservations, later studies confirm the basic accuracy of Kaplan's observations; see, for example, Fan Shen's comments on the structure of Chinese discourse (Shen, 1989, pp. 462–465) and Shirley Ostler's on discourse in English by Arabic speakers (Ostler, 1987).

2. Kaplan provides a useful overview of work in contrastive rhetoric in "Contrastive Rhetoric and Second Language Learning: Notes Toward a Theory of Contrastive Rhetoric" (Kaplan, 1988). Among the recently published collections of work in contrastive rhetoric are those edited by Ulla Connor and Robert B. Kaplan (*Writing across Languages: Analysis of L2 Text,* 1987) and by Alan C. Purves (*Writing across Languages and Cultures,* 1988).

3. Heath cautions that portaits like the ones synthesized here should not be considered definitive. They are derived from extended observations in particular families, and have been verified by members of the groups involved to be consistent with their own experience and their knowledge of the culture. Nonetheless, Heath notes that "within the next few years, the publications of research currently underway by these and other scholars will, no doubt, both alter and greatly augment these beginning efforts to describe the sociocultural foundations of language development among the language minorities of California" (1986, p. 160).

HELPING LANGUAGE MINORITY STUDENTS READ AND WRITE ANALYTICALLY: THE JOURNEY INTO, THROUGH, AND BEYOND

Donna Brinton ■ *Janet Goodwin* ■ *Laura Ranks*

When faced with challenging texts, language minority students experience quite predictable hurdles. They may not know how to process what they read and may not share the writer's implicit cultural assumptions. Depending on the level of their English proficiency, they may also lack familiarity with the vocabulary and structural elements of the text. This chapter proposes an instructional method, the "into, through, and beyond" model, which is designed to maximize student access to challenging text."[1] Though designed initially for use in California's literature-enriched language arts curriculum, this model can be adapted by language and content teachers alike, and can be applied to a large variety of texts—both those of the language and literature class and those of the content class.

"Into, through, and beyond" describes the journey we guide our students on in order to discover meaning in a text. This model offers teachers a way to help their students to approach a text (*into*), interact with it (*through*), and write an analytical response to it (*beyond*). The underlying assumption here is that only through clearly established connections will the reader generate the associations, inferences, and abstractions necessary to formulate a reasoned response. Analytical thinking is the product of this active dialogue between the reader and the writer. At the end of this journey, students reflect on where they have been and discover their relationship to the voyage they have taken.

GETTING INTO THE TEXT

The "into" phase allows students the opportunity to approach a text's content without yet interacting with the writing itself. In this phase of the process, students explore a topic or theme and, with their teacher's guidance, find out what they already know about it. We believe that only when these connections between the students' own life experiences and the theme or topic of the work have been established can language minority students make meaning of the written text.

To initiate this process, teachers must anticipate the connections a student might have to a given piece of writing and find ways to bring that knowledge alive. The activities in this phase may involve any of the four skill areas—listening, speaking, reading, and writing—and should take into consideration the variety of learning styles students may have. This beginning, which establishes a comfortable relationship between the reader and the ideas contained in a piece, is crucial if the reader's dialogue with the writer is to be opened and sustained.

Typical "into" activities include the following: visual stimuli (i.e., magazine pictures) which stimulate students to discuss the central theme of the text to be read; journal prompts or quickwrites in which students are asked to share prior personal experiences on the theme or topic; vocabulary clustering activities in which the students' lexical boundaries vis-a-vis the topic are explored and expanded; values clarification exercises, often in the form of anticipation/reaction guides or closure exercises, which ask students to identify and crystallize their attitudes on a topic; and free association or visualization exercises that introduce students to the context of the text to be read and allow them to imagine themselves in this context. Examples of these activities will be found in the sample unit that follows.

WORKING THROUGH THE TEXT

Once students' prior knowledge and personal experience of the topic have been brought to the fore, the next step—*through*—is to promote each reader's active interaction with the text. Just as a listener asks questions of a conversational partner, the successful reader poses his own questions in a silent dialogue with the writer. To emphasize the active nature of this communication between the reader and writer, the teacher designs activities to foster students' ability to comprehend the text and to relate the writer's ideas to his or her own. The reading process is again supplemented by both speaking and writing activities.

If the text is long, it can be helpful to work with only a part of it at one time. For example, the teacher can take a single paragraph (narrative or chronological ones work well) and cut it into sentence strips. Each student in a group receives one sentence and together the students reconstruct the logical sequence. This may be done with successive paragraphs in a text as well. Topic sentences of paragraphs can be used to predict the content of the paragraph or a single paragraph can be used to anticipate the following ones.

A "jigsaw" reading activity is another method of dividing the text into manageable chunks for students. In this technique, students are divided into "expert" groups—each of which has one part of the complete text. By answering guide questions, looking for the main idea, listing and defining key vocabulary, and so on, each group becomes expert on its section of the text. Once this is accomplished, new groups are formed; each new group consists of one expert from each of the former groups. With these new panels of "experts" the text may be reconstructed into its whole, with each member contributing his or her part. Then the teacher can set new tasks that require a knowledge of the integrated whole rather than the individual parts, promoting cooperation within the group.

Another way of working through the text is to highlight key passages and have students write about their context and meaning in a T-graph format. One can also have students focus on lexical choice in a given passage—either by asking them to collect words in a given semantic field or by giving them paraphrases of important passages in the text and asking them to find the originals. These activities encourage students to pay close attention to the language of the text as well as its message.

MOVING BEYOND THE TEXT

"Through" strategies are designed to enable students to grasp the meaning of a text as they read through it. Moving beyond the text, readers then reflect on what they have received from it, establish a clear voice and response, and themselves become writers. In this stage—*beyond*—the dialogue with the author of the text is completed as the new written response unfolds.

"Beyond" activities that assist students in processing the text include class or group discussions, as well as interviews with people outside the class who can offer additional insight on the ideas presented in the work. In general, the more students have a chance to "talk through" the text and reinterpret its meaning in their own terms, the better equipped they will be able to articulate its central ideas when asked to put these in writing. For this purpose, role play and dramatization also work well, especially when dealing with literary texts. By actually performing key scenes from the work, limited English proficient students are better able to understand the motives of a particular character, and thus come closer to understanding the author's overall intent.

Writing activities at this phase may be of two types, both valuable—preanalytical or analytical. Preanalytical writing activities may take the form of journal responses to ideas in the text, or other more personal forms of writing. With literary texts, for example, the preanalytical writing activity might take the form of getting the students to write from the point of view of one of the work's characters. Thus students might be asked to imagine that the scene has shifted to five years in the future, and be asked to write about their (i.e., the character's) life at this point in time. Or they might be asked to assume the role of a more minor character in the work and describe a key scene from this point of view. A novel technique that involves student pairs is the "silent dialogue." In this activity, each student receives a description of a new situation and assumes the role of a specific character. Using one sheet of paper, the students take turns creating the dialogue between these characters—on paper and without a word being spoken. This dialogue is then generally performed for the group or class.

The final task for students is to write an analytical response to the text according to the prompt set by the teacher. In this prompt, the student is often asked to put together the critical thinking skills practiced in the unit by summarizing the reading and reacting to it. The reaction part of the response goes beyond the summary by asking the student to evaluate the writer's ideas and relate them to the student's own personal and world knowledge. This step is an essential one in promoting the student's ability to think analytically and communicate ideas effectively.

SAMPLE UNIT: INVESTIGATING THE THEMES OF DISCRIMINATION AND PREJUDICE THROUGH THE AUTOBIOGRAPHY AND NOVEL GENRES

For this sample unit, which is designed for high school students about to be mainstreamed, we have chosen extracts from an essay by Bruno Bettelheim and from the novel *Ragtime* by E. L. Doctorow. While these two works are literary in nature and the audience they anticipate is relatively proficient in English, the techniques of the into, through, and beyond model illustrated in this unit are adaptable to other levels of proficiency, and to other types of texts as well.[2]

The passages we have chosen for this unit deal with the experiences of Bruno Bettelheim, a Jewish psychologist interned in a Nazi labor camp, and Coalhouse Walker, *Ragtime*'s African-American protagonist, who is a successful musician in New York City at the beginning of this century. At the core of this unit is the integration of the two genres, memoir and novel, both of which present students with the central characters' experiences of prejudice and portray their reactions to the treatment they receive at the hands of their oppressors. For the passages themselves, please see Appendix A.[3]

The sample class activities discussed in the opening section are designed to lead students from a spontaneous response to a critical or analytical reaction. Outlined below are a number of suggested activities in each of the three phases of the lesson. We are not suggesting that any teacher would or could use all of these activities with any one reading. We have compiled this variety so that teachers can choose those activities that they feel most comfortable with and that they believe would be most helpful given their own students' profiles. Similarly, we are not recommending that teachers use the Bettelheim/Walker unit in their own classes, though they are welcome to do so;[4] rather, we hope that teachers will find exemplified here new ways of using text more interactively in their own classes, and that these activities will suggest ways that they can stimulate and challenge their students. Figure 4.1 introduces the variety of activities in the units.[5]

PHASE ONE: LEADING STUDENTS INTO THE TEXT

All of the activities in this section focus on personal experience, a powerful means of focusing student attention. Each activity asks the students to reflect on incidents of prejudice in their own lives, or on their thoughts and feelings about situations involving discrimination they have observed. Many of the

INTO
1. Clustering activity—"Discrimination" word wheel
2. Visualization—Being imprisoned
3. Journal prompt—Experience with prejudice
4. Song—"We Shall Overcome"
5. Closure exercise
6. Anticipation/reaction guide

THROUGH
1. Strip story/sentence strip activity
2. Vocabulary collecting—Star diagram
3. Jigsaw reading
4. Vocabulary collecting—Star diagram
5. Paraphrase activity
6. Vocabulary building—Personal characteristics
7. Vocabulary building—Character analysis
8. T-graph—Text interpretation
9. T-graph—Text interpretation
10. Identifying sources
11. Illustrating quotations
12. Venn diagram—Character comparison

BEYOND
1. Writing a letter home
2. Silent dialogue
3. Dramatization
4. Analytical essay

Figure 4.1. Activities in the Bettelheim/Walker Unit

exercises can lead to "quick writes" in their journals; all are designed to build bridges to the passages they will read. Through recalling their own feelings, students are encouraged/enabled to identify with the experiences of the characters in the literary pieces and the central themes their authors are presenting. We suggest that teachers select two or three of the "into" activities to use before students read the texts.

Clustering Activity—"Discrimination" Word Wheel

Activity 1

Rationale: This is a potent method for examining many dimensions of a subject. It involves the whole class and gives the individual students material to help recall incidents from personal experience. This leads to richer writing.

Procedure: For this blackboard clustering activity, write the word *discrimination* in capitals in the center of the blackboard, circle it, and draw lines emanating out from the circle or word wheel. Ask students the following question, writing the ideas elicited next to the lines:

What kinds of things do you believe that people discriminate against?

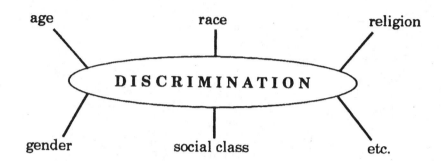

Following completion of the word wheel, ask students to brainstorm incidents of discrimination that they have observed or experienced. These can serve as a basis for Activity 3, the journal prompt.

Activity 2

Visualization—Being Imprisoned

Rationale: Guided visualization stirs the imagination and is a very powerful tool for recreating experience. Students may need to be taught the techniques of visualization. Closing the eyes to see pictures may not come easily to some students, and they may need practice to be comfortable.

As this was being written, Frank Herbert Reed, an American hostage in Lebanon, had just been released. He was blindfolded 24 hours a day and chained to a wall for two years. Students might examine what that experience would be like—to be totally isolated inside the self.

Procedure: Teachers can read the following visualization exercise aloud to students, writing the words elicited from students on the blackboard and clustering like lexical sets together. Follow-up discussion should ensue. Note that this works best with lights dimmed and students seated in a circle or in a relaxed posture. Appropriate background music (i.e., film soundtrack) helps too! *Note:* Some teachers may feel uncomfortable using this specific guided visualization because of experiences that their students or their students' families may have had in the past and may therefore opt not to use the activity.

VISUALIZATION EXERCISE: BEING IMPRISONED

Close your eyes. Imagine yourself in jail, far away from your family members and unable to communicate with them. You are totally alone in your small, dark jail cell, and have no contact with your fellow prisoners. What are your innermost feelings? What conditions are you encountering? Be specific—what sounds, smells, sights do you experience?

Activity
3

Journal Prompt—Experience with Prejudice

Rationale: Even more directly than the clustering activity, this activity enables students to reflect on personal experiences or observations that relate to the themes they are about to encounter in the literary works. It also gives them a chance to use their personal voice to articulate these thoughts on paper.

Procedure: Use the following prompt for student journal entries or as an in-class writing activity (quickwrite).

Have you ever experienced prejudice? You can write about an event you witnessed or one where you personally were the victim of prejudice. What do you think the cause of this prejudice was?

STUDENT SAMPLE

When we wanted to come to America we went to Damgham to get visa, because there is an American embassy in Iran. I already had American passport because I had born here but my family needed to get visa. In the embassy employees had a bad behaviour to persians. I couldn't believe it. They were shouting and insulting persians. When it was our turn to enter to embassy and the employee saw my American passport and found that I'm American, he changed his behaviour. He acted so polite to my family because there was an American person in our family. I got a bad feeling inside myself. They act to people politely if they are American. They don't look at people as humans.

Activity
4

Song—"We Shall Overcome"

Rationale: "We Shall Overcome" is an important cultural milestone of the American Civil Rights movement and relates closely to the theme of racial prejudice.

Procedure: The song "We Shall Overcome" can be either sung or played in class, with lyrics distributed to students. The teacher should set the cultural context of the song by giving some background to the civil rights movement and explaining that the word *overcome* here refers to overcoming experiences of discrimination and achieving racial equality. Teachers may wish to use an audiotaped version of the songs or to play a segment of video to further acquaint students with the civil rights movement. To this end, we suggest the PBS series "Eyes on the Prize." Students can also be asked to share other songs that deal with discrimination or prejudice.

WE SHALL OVERCOME

We shall overcome, we shall overcome
We shall overcome some day.
Oh, deep in my heart
I do believe
We shall overcome some day.

We'll walk hand in hand (3x) some day
Oh deep in my heart . . . some day.

We are not afraid (3x) today
Oh deep in my heart . . . some day.

We shall live in peace (3x) some day
Oh deep in my heart . . . some day.

Truth will make us free (3x) some day
Oh deep in my heart . . . some day.

We shall brothers be (3x) some day
Oh deep in my heart . . . some day.

Black and white together (3x) some day
Oh deep in my heart . . . some day.

American protest song
Civil rights movement, 1960s

Activity 5

Closure Exercise

Rationale: This exercise probes the student's experience of personal discrimination and creates a bridge to the central theme of the two texts in this unit.

Procedure: Individually (probably as homework), have students complete the closure exercise below. Students can then be grouped to share their answers, and class discussion can ensue.

CLOSURE EXERCISE

Instructions to Students: Finish each of the phrases below with your own words.

1. People make fun of a person because _____

_____

2. I feel I am mistreated when _____

_____

3. Being an ESL student means _____

_____

4. When I am treated differently than other people I feel _____

_____

5. Some people in the United States say that they are mistreated because

_____

6. The unique thing about living in the United States is _____

_____

7. People come to understand persons of different races because _____

_____

8. Since I don't speak English perfectly, I feel _____

_____

9. We will understand people better if _____

_____

10. The biggest problem I had to solve after coming to the United States was

_____

<table>
<tr><td>**Activity**
6</td></tr>
</table>

Anticipation/Reaction Guide

Rationale: Examining attitudes before reading and contrasting them with attitudes after reading make students aware of the power of text. Seeing with different eyes, one often modifies opinions and gains insight. Changing and broadening attitudes are among the major purposes of this unit.

Procedure: The anticipation/reaction guide below should be used as a pre- and postreading exercise. Prior to reading the Bettelheim/Walker selections, ask students individually to check off the left-hand column of the worksheet with their personal reactions. Then, following the reading of the passage, ask them to check off the right-hand column. Students will discuss any changes of opinion.

ANTICIPATION/REACTION GUIDE

Instructions to Students:

A. Before reading: Check *agree* or *disagree* for each of the following statements in the left-hand column.

B. After reading: Check *agree* or *disagree* for each of the following statements in the right-hand column.

Agree	Disagree		Agree	Disagree
_____	_____	1. People who suffer often deserve the treatment they get.	_____	_____
_____	_____	2. You can always get help from a policeman.	_____	_____
_____	_____	3. Manipulation is better than resistance.	_____	_____
_____	_____	4. There is often good reason to mistrust people of different races or ethnicities.	_____	_____
_____	_____	5. Everyone responds to human suffering by offering to help.	_____	_____
_____	_____	6. People who have more than other people are more able to take care of themselves.	_____	_____
_____	_____	7. Justice comes when a case is argued clearly.	_____	_____
_____	_____	8. Certain ethnic groups have too much power and influence.	_____	_____
_____	_____	9. Minority group members should be kept in their place in society and should not overstep their bounds.	_____	_____
_____	_____	10. Through history, we have learned from the mistakes of the past.	_____	_____

These "through" activities focus on the texts themselves and lead students to close reading. The emphasis shifts to the authors—what they have to say, what their purposes are. Now the student is involved in unlocking meaning. Most of the activities use graphic organizers to make abstract ideas visual and concrete and thus more easily understood.

<table>
<tr><td>Activity
1</td></tr>
</table>

Strip Story/Sentence Strip Activity

Rationale: By reconstructing a key paragraph from the text in proper sentence order, the student experiences directly the ways in which the author creates meaning. This heightens anticipation of the story, which students have not yet read in its entirety, and sharpens reading skills.

Procedure:

1. *Alternative 1*—Strip story exercise: On index cards, type the following sentences, adapted slightly from the Coalhouse Walker passage. Students can then be given a brief introduction to the story (see below) and formed into groups of eight, asked to form circles, and then asked to read their sentences aloud without showing them to the other members of the circle. Their goal is to rearrange themselves so that the sentences are in the correct order. (Alternately, one group of eight volunteers can perform the activity in the front of the class, with the other students acting as a live audience.) The sentences should be shuffled before distributing them to the students. Once students have completed the task, they can write the sentences in correct order on the board or on the overhead projector for further discussion.

2. *Alternative 2*—Sentence strip exercise: In this case, each sentence of the key paragraph should be typed on a strip of paper. Each group of students is given the background to the story and the sentence strips (in jumbled order); groups are then asked to rearrange these sentences in proper narrative order. This adaptation of the activity may be more appropriate for students whose listening skills are weak, or for classes where teachers wish to focus on coherence in written discourse.

3. *Follow-up*—For either of the above alternatives, here are some suggested follow-up questions for discussion:
    a. From this excerpt, what can you tell about Coalhouse Walker's personality?
    b. What do you think of the firemen's demand? Is it justified? Why or why not?
    c. Do you think Coalhouse will get assistance at the police station?
    d. What do you think will happen when Coalhouse returns to his car?

Background: Coalhouse Walker is a character in the novel *Ragtime,* set in New York City at the beginning of this century. He is a successful black musician; he drives an expensive car and dresses elegantly. He is aware that because of his wealth, he provokes many white people.

Coalhouse Walker's trip back to New York took him past a company of volunteer firemen.

As he drove along, a team of three horses pulled a fire engine into the road ahead of him and stopped, blocking the road.

The firemen advised Walker that he could not drive on without paying a $25 toll.

"This is a public thoroughfare," Walker said. "I've traveled it dozens of times and no one has ever said anything about a toll."

The Fire Chief explained that while the toll had never been collected, it was nevertheless in force.

Walker decided to back up and go another way.

At this moment, however, several firemen carried out ladders and other equipment, all of which they set down behind Walker's car.

Coalhouse considered the courses of action available to him. Apparently it did not occur to him to ingratiate himself.

Instead, he asked two black teenagers to watch his car. He then walked back to the police office in the town's business district.

Vocabulary Collecting—Star Diagram

Activity 2

Rationale: These diagrams can be used in several ways. The example here asks students to analyze the text by discovering the elements that create meaning. This visual presentation clarifies the "who, what, when, and where" aspects of the piece.

Procedure: Star diagrams, which require students to select vocabulary from the work and categorize it, work best as a small-group activity. Distribute the handouts to students, then have them locate and write appropriate vocabulary words next to the points of the star diagram. Once the groups are finished with the activity, they can share the vocabulary they have collected.

VOCABULARY COLLECTING: STAR DIAGRAM

Instructions to Students: Reread the passage from *Ragtime* about Coalhouse Walker. As you read, collect the words and phrases that relate to the categories in the star diagram below. Write these phrases next to the points of the star. An example of each category has already been done for you. (The following is an example of one student's star diagram.)

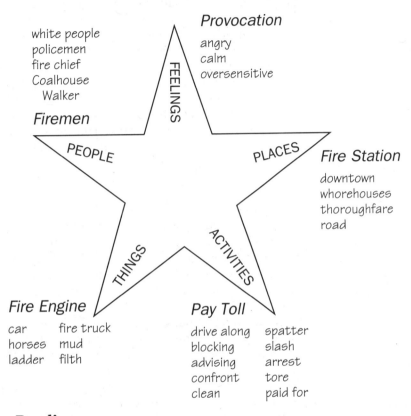

Provocation
angry
calm
oversensitive

white people
policemen
fire chief
Coalhouse
  Walker
Firemen

FEELINGS

PEOPLE

PLACES

Fire Station
downtown
whorehouses
thoroughfare
road

Fire Engine
car   fire truck
horses   mud
ladder   filth

THINGS

ACTIVITIES

Pay Toll
drive along   spatter
blocking   slash
advising   arrest
confront   tore
clean   paid for

<table>
<tr><td>Activity
3</td></tr>
</table>

Jigsaw Reading

Rationale: The Bruno Bettelheim passage lends itself nicely to jigsaw reading. Each member of the class becomes a "teacher" in this exercise. It is an effective teaching tool in several ways: Students have the support of a peer group, called their "expert" group, as they locate the main ideas in their assigned paragraphs, and they also have teaching responsibility to deliver the central meaning of one paragraph to the home group in which they begin and end the activity. This exercise guarantees participation of each member of the class. Because of the time required, choose for this activity paragraphs central to the meaning of the text.

Materials: Butcher paper or extra large tablet and four large colored pens for each group.

Procedures:

1. Create three even groups of students. For example, in a class of 18, three groups of 6 students each would be formed. For the more typical high school class of 36, create two parallel sets of groups. These groups are the "home groups" into which students will later reassemble.

2. Assign each student in the home group a letter (A, B, or C) and have students regroup into new configurations or "expert groups," with Group A assembling in one corner, Group B in another corner, and Group C in a third corner. In this new configuration, for example, Group A would be comprised of two "A" students from Home Group 1, two "A" students from Home Group 2, and two "A" students from Home Group 3.

3. Assign paragraphs to the various groups without disclosing details about their sequential ordering. The three paragraphs of the text along with possible discussion questions follow these procedures.

   Expert Group A: Paragraph 1

   Expert Group B: Paragraph 2

   Expert Group C: Paragraph 3

4. Students read the assigned paragraph, underlining any unknown vocabulary and checking on its definition by first asking group members for meaning, and then (as a last resort) looking these words up in the dictionary. The teacher can circulate from group to group during this time helping out as needed. Each group of students will determine the main ideas in the paragraphs and write these on butcher paper. They should be encouraged to illustrate these pages to further clarify the main points.

5. The butcher paper summaries are hung around the room for easy reference and students are regrouped into their original groups. In this way, "experts" on each paragraph share what they know with the home group to reconstruct the text.

6. In their home groups, students orally share the main essence of their original paragraphs with the other members of their group, referring to their butcher paper guides as necessary. At this point, students should not refer back to the original text. In this fashion, each student becomes a teacher. Together, they determine the correct sequential order of the paragraphs.

7. After all the paragraphs have been discussed, the teacher asks the students to generalize the main idea of the passage. This can be summarized on the blackboard.

8. Finally, the entire passage is handed out to students to be read as homework.

Paragraph for Expert Group A

No Jewish prisoner ahead of me in the line was admitted to the clinic. The more a prisoner pleaded, the more annoyed and violent the SS private became. Expressions of pain amused him; stories of previous services rendered to Germany outraged him. He proudly remarked that he could not be taken in by Jews, and fortunately the time had passed when Jews could reach their goals by lamentations.

Paragraph for Expert Group B

When my turn came, he asked me in a screeching voice if I knew that work accidents were the only reason for admitting Jews to the clinic, and if I came because of such an accident. I replied that I knew the rules, but that I couldn't work unless my hands were freed of the dead flesh. Since prisoners were not allowed to have knives, I asked to have the dead flesh cut away. I tried to be matter-of-fact, avoiding pleading, deference, or arrogance. He replied: "If that's all you want, I'll tear the flesh off myself." And he started to pull at the festering skin. Because it did not come off as easily as he may have expected, or for some other reason, he waved me into the clinic.

Paragraph for Expert Group C

Inside, he gave me an angry look and pushed me into the treatment room. There he told the prisoner orderly to attend to the wound. While this was being done, the guard watched me closely for signs of pain, but I was able to suppress them. As soon as the cutting was over, I started to leave. The guard showed surprise and asked why I didn't wait for further treatment. I said I had gotten the service I had asked for, at which he told the orderly to make an exception and treat my hand. After I had left the room, he called me back and gave me a card entitling me to further treatment, and admittance to the clinic without inspection at the entrance.

Directions to give students when they've moved from home groups to expert groups:

Stage 1: You should be in your "expert" groups—"A", "B", or "C." Read the passage you just received. Once you have finished reading your "piece" of the passage, discuss it with your group, and answer the questions below to the best of your ability.

Which piece of the jigsaw do you think you have—the beginning, middle, or end?

Is this reading fact or fiction? Why?

What time period does the reading take place in?

What kind of man is the main character? What event(s) give you clues to his character?

What other main character(s) are there? Are they sympathetic or not?

Stage 2: Members from the original home groups should now be assembled together. Share your piece of the puzzle with the other members of the group. You should attempt to reconstruct the entire episode. Once you have completed this task, answer the following questions:

What surprised you the most about the other pieces of the passage?

How do the narrator's experiences relate to the present time period? Could a situation like the one that is related exist today?

If you were to give this piece a title, what would you call it?

Would you want to read more by this same author? Why/why not?

Vocabulary Collecting—Star Diagram

Activity 4

Rationale: This star diagram asks the students to collect vocabulary that is relevant to certain aspects of the text. This exercise expands vocabulary acquisition while it assists students in unlocking meaning.

Procedure: The star diagram activity discussed earlier can be easily adapted for the Bruno Bettelheim passage. See the example below.

Vocabulary Collecting: Star Diagram

Instructions to Students: Reread the Bettelheim passage. As you read, collect the words and phrases which relate to the categories in the star diagram below. Write these phrases next to the points of the star. An example of each category has already been done for you. (A student sample follows.)

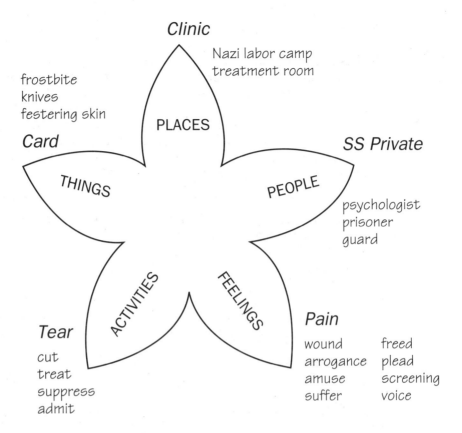

Clinic

Nazi labor camp
treatment room

frostbite
knives
festering skin

PLACES

Card

THINGS

SS Private

PEOPLE

psychologist
prisoner
guard

Tear

ACTIVITIES

FEELINGS

cut
treat
suppress
admit

Pain

wound   freed
arrogance   plead
amuse   screening
suffer   voice

Paraphrase Activity

Rationale: Presenting students with paraphrases of passages they have already read helps them to gain an appreciation for the richness of the English language and to grasp more concretely the meaning of the original passages. Presenting students with paraphrases in this fashion is a necessary precedent to asking them to write their own paraphrases of passages—a skill that requires much practice on their part.

Procedure: This exercise is a particularly challenging one, as it requires that students understand the meaning of *paraphrase*. It is also challenging since it involves both passages and because students need to use their knowledge of both works to locate the relevant passages. Teachers would be well advised to do the first paraphrase activity below with the group as a whole, and to discuss with their students the importance of paraphrase in their own writing. Before locating the original passage, students might be asked to volunteer possible alternatives for the underlined words in number 1. Teachers may also lead them to discuss the subtle differences in meaning between the words used in the paraphrase and those used in the original text (i.e., *angry* vs. *annoyed*). Numbers 2–5 should be done in small groups, with results then shared with the class as a whole.

Paraphrase Activity

Instructions to Students: The following five sentences represent central ideas from the Coalhouse Walker and Bruno Bettelheim readings. However, these sentences do not use the original words of the authors; instead, they are paraphrases of the original passage. For each paraphrase below, locate the original passage from either the Bettelheim or Walker reading and write it below the paraphrase. Notice that some words in the paraphrase are underlined. Locate the corresponding words in the original text and underline them as well. What other changes do you notice in the passages?

---

1. Paraphrase: If one of the <u>captives</u> <u>begged for</u> <u>mercy,</u> the <u>officer</u> became <u>angry</u> and <u>cruel.</u>

Original Text:

2. Paraphrase: They don't <u>intend to</u> cause any <u>damage</u>. <u>In all likelihood</u>, they have <u>lost interest</u> and aren't <u>amused</u> any more.

Original Text:

3. Paraphrase: <u>Throughout</u> the past, he had <u>dealt</u> <u>with</u> these <u>sentiments</u>.

Original Text:

4. Paraphrase: Once we had entered, he <u>glared</u> at me and <u>shoved</u> me into the <u>examining</u> room.

Original Text:

5. Paraphrase: <u>Set</u> in the <u>rear</u> seat of the car was a <u>pile</u> of <u>human waste.</u>

Original Text:

<table>
<tr><td>**Activity 6**</td></tr>
</table>

Vocabulary Building—Personal Characteristics

Rationale: This exercise provides students with a set of vocabulary items useful for comparing and contrasting the characteristics of the protagonists in the two pieces. Understanding the personalities of the characters is central to unlocking meaning in these pieces.

Procedure: During this small-group in-class activity, the teacher should circulate and explain the meaning of the adjectives for personal characteristics as needed. Alternately, students can be directed to use their dictionaries as needed.

PERSONAL CHARACTERISTICS

Instructions to Students: Read the Bruno Bettelheim and Coalhouse Walker passages. Then, look at the words in the box. You may use a dictionary if you wish. Decide which characteristics belong to Bettelheim and which ones belong to Walker. List the adjectives in the spaces below each name. You may want to use the same word to describe both characters.

Bettelheim   Walker

_____   sensitive   honest   brave   _____

_____   persuasive   patient   _____

_____   thoughtful   forthright   _____

_____

Can you think of any other words to describe the personalities of Bettelheim or Walker? Write them below.

Bettelheim   Walker

_____   _____

_____   _____

_____   _____

_____   _____

_____   _____

_____   _____

_____

Activity 7

Vocabulary Building—Character Analysis

Rationale: As in the previous activity, students are provided with the vocabulary necessary to make comparisons between the central characters.

However, here they are also given a graphic organizer that helps them to compare Bettelheim and Walker visually.

Procedure: Like the previous one, this activity lends itself to in-class discussion of the two main characters. To prepare for the discussion, distribute the handout to students as an in-class small-group activity or for homework. Again, allow students to use their dictionaries as needed.

CHARACTER ANALYSIS

Instructions to Students: Decide whether you think the two characters have a high or a low amount of the qualities named at the left. Use an X for Bettelheim and an O for Walker, and show how you think the two characters compare with each other by placing the letters on the lines between "high" "and low." If you aren't sure, leave it blank.

deference   LOW————————————————————————————HIGH

sensitivity   LOW————————————————————————————HIGH

anxiety   LOW————————————————————————————HIGH

independence   LOW————————————————————————————HIGH

arrogance   LOW————————————————————————————HIGH

openness   LOW————————————————————————————HIGH

intelligence   LOW————————————————————————————HIGH

Activity 8

T-Graph—Text Interpretation

Rationale: Determining the inner meanings of a text can be very challenging for language minority students. By isolating small units in this way, we focus on important ideas they might otherwise not focus on, and we make close reading much less threatening.

Procedure: The T-graph activity again lends itself either to use in class or as homework. Students are asked to give their own interpretation for key passages from the Coalhouse Walker text.

T-GRAPH ACTIVITY

Instructions to Students: Sometimes people say things that have a meaning that's not obvious. Each of the quotes below from the Coalhouse Walker passage carries an extra message. Locate the quotation in the text and look at the context in which it occurs. Then, in your own words, interpret this message.

Quotation from the Text	Your Interpretation
1. "This is a public thoroughfare."	1.
2. "They don't mean no harm."	2.
3. ". . . you be on your way."	3.
4. "There's no real damage done."	4.
5. "I was on my way when they stopped me."	5.

Activity 9

T-Graph—Text Interpretation

Procedure: Similarly, the T-graph format can be adapted to the Bruno Bettelheim passage.

T-GRAPH ACTIVITY

Instructions to Students: Sometimes people say things that have a meaning that's not obvious. Each of the quotations below from the Bruno Bettelheim passage carries an extra message. Locate the quote in the text and look at the context in which it occurs. Then in your own words, interpret this message.

Quotation from the Text	Your Interpretation
1. "[The SS private] proudly remarked that he could not be taken in by Jews. . ."	1.
2. ". . . fortunately the time had passed when Jews could reach their goals by lamentations."	2.

continued on next page

3. "I tried to be matter-of-fact,
avoiding pleading, deference,
or arrogance."   3.

4. "I said I had gotten the service   4.
I had asked for. . ."

Identifying Sources

Rationale: By asking students to identify the sources and contexts of key
quotations, we are focusing their attention on differences in attitude, motivation,
feeling, and opinion. This forced choice activity helps students sort out any
remaining confusion they might have about the work.

Procedure: This activity can again be done in small groups during class time
or as an out-of-class activity, assigned as homework.

IDENTIFYING SOURCES

Instructions to Students: Which character—Bettelheim or Walker—said or
thought the following things? Put an X in the appropriate spaces below.

	Bettelheim	Walker
1. "I replied that I knew the rules. . ."	___	___
2. "I tried to be matter-of-fact, avoiding pleading, deference, or arrogance."	___	___
3. "I was on my way when they stopped me."	___	___
4. I was able to suppress signs of pain.	___	___
5. ". . . I want an apology."	___	___
6. "I do not drink."	___	___
7. "I said I had gotten the service I had asked for. . ."	___	___
8. All my life I had coped with such feelings.	___	___

Can you remember the circumstances in which these quotations occurred? Find the quotations in the text and check your answers.

Illustrating Quotations

Rationale: This activity allows students to select their own key quotations from the materials they have read and to illustrate these quotations. Thus students are encouraged to exercise their own judgments of significance, an important step toward awakening in them a critical awareness. If students can make an idea visual, they usually have grasped it thoroughly and will remember it.

Materials: Butcher paper, colored pens and pencils, glue and scissors, miscellaneous source materials (i.e., magazines, construction paper, etc.)

Procedure: In small groups or individually, students are asked to select a quotation from the work that they have just read and to illustrate it, either using freehand illustration or collage techniques. This can be done as an in-class or out-of-class activity, depending on the teacher's preference. Once students have finished the posters, they present them to their classmates and explain their choices. The posters can be hung around the classroom to make subsequent class discussion more meaningful.

Venn Diagram

Rationale: This activity makes the similarities and differences between the two main characters in the pieces very clear visually. Building on the information students have gathered in the other comparison-contrast exercises, it makes a good culminating activity for this stage of the students' literary journey.

Procedure: A Venn diagram provides a useful tool for students to compare the two characters and graphically map out their similarities and differences. This can be done either as a blackboard brainstorming activity or with the students configured in small groups.

Instructions to Students: Coalhouse Walker and Bruno Bettelheim share a similar experience—they are victims of prejudice. However, they react in somewhat different ways to this experience. To what extent do you think these two men share similar characteristics? To what extent do they differ in personality? Write the shared characteristics where the two circles intersect.

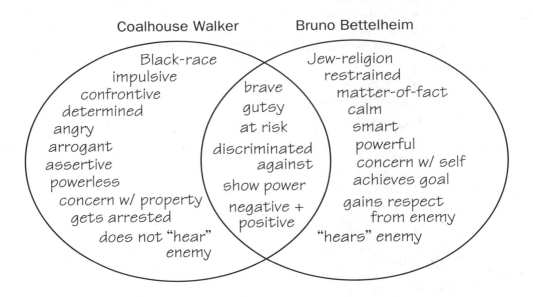

Student Sample

PHASE THREE: LEADING STUDENTS BEYOND THE TEXT

The purpose of the "beyond" activities is synthesis. Once the students have unlocked meaning in the pieces and have seen relationships between the experiences of these characters and their own experience, they are ready to synthesize these ideas and use them to create their own pieces of analytical writing. These activities use the reading as a foundation and ask the student to become a writer.

Activity 1

Writing a Letter Home

Rationale: This activity requires the student to delve into the personality of the literary figure and, in essence, to become that person. This personalized writing allows students to examine—from within—the motivations and conflicts; later, students will be asked to examine these characters from a distance.

Procedure: In this writing task, students assume the role of either Bruno Bettelheim or Coalhouse Walker. Before asking students to write the letter, the teacher should brainstorm with students—asking them, for example, what kinds of things men write in letters to their wives, what they would be apt to describe in their letters, whether they would want their wives to know about their suffering, and so on.

WRITING A LETTER HOME

Instructions to Students: For this exercise you can choose to be either Bettelheim or Walker. You are writing a letter to your wife, who cannot visit you because you are imprisoned. Will the character you have chosen be truthful about the conditions he is experiencing, or will he protect his wife from this information? Will he show his anger and frustration, or hide it and pretend that all is well?

(today's date)

My dearest wife,

Much love,

STUDENT SAMPLE

My Dearest wife,

I know it has been a long time since the last time I wrote. I am very sorry I didn't have the chance to write earlier. I was in a very bad condition and I did not have the time and the nerves to write. I don't want to worry you too much. The important part is that I am fine now. I miss you too much, though, I wish I was at home with you forever. I am happy, in a way, that you are not here because I don't want you to experience what I did. I don't want you to see how the SS soldiers are treating the Jews. It is a very sad scene. Women and children are crying for help. They are pleading for help and nobody seems to hear them. I am glad that I am the only one that is going through this and the children and you are not. I hope you are not taking it too hard on yourself. Enjoy your life and think positive. Yes, that is all we have to do, think positive. I am sure it will be over soon and when it will we will be together again forever. Don't give up, darling, you are a strong woman. With your encouragement and love and mine we will get over it. Tears are coming to my eyes when I write this paper. I just can't accept the fact that I am not with you and did not have the chance to see Isaac grow. I would love to hear from you. Tell me what you went through. Is Sara o.k.? How the children are doing in school? Give my love to them and tell them to write a few words to their father who loves you and them very very much.

> Take Care
> and
> Much Love.
> Bruno

<table>
<tr><td>Activity
2</td></tr>
</table>

Silent Dialogue

Rationale: Like the preceding activity, this one provides students with writing practice that grows out of the literary experience and expands on it. It also provides students with practice in making relevant responses to items in "spoken discourse," and helps them enter into the personality and thought processes of the characters in the texts they are reading.

Procedure: Assign roles to pairs of students, as outlined below. Each role should be written on an index card. Difficult words should be explained. The paired students share a piece of paper on which the silent dialogue is to be written. After they have written the dialogue, they can share it by reading it aloud to the other students.

SILENT DIALOGUE

Instructions to Students: Your job is to write a "silent dialogue" between two characters in the works of literature you have been reading. You will see that the characters are now in a new situation. You will write this dialogue on a piece of paper that you pass back and forth. No talking is allowed. If your character's name has an asterisk (*) before it, you should begin writing the dialogue. After you have finished writing the dialogue, you may want to go back and make some changes. Once you are satisfied with the results, you'll be asked to read your dialogue aloud to the class and to defend or explain the statements you've written.

SILENT DIALOGUE 1

*Bruno Bettelheim: Because your hands have swollen badly since your last visit to the clinic, you decide to use the card given to you by the prisoner orderly. Again, you don't want special treatment; you just want the wounds lanced so you can return to work.

Prisoner orderly: Bruno Bettelheim, the prisoner who was treated for dead flesh on his hands last week, returns to your clinic using the card you gave him for admittance. Instead of healing, his hands have become seriously infected, and are swollen to almost twice their normal size. Bettelheim looks feverish and appears to have no strength. You feel he needs antibiotics and should be admitted for several days to the clinic.

SILENT DIALOGUE 2

*Coalhouse Walker: As a result of the incident with your car, you've been placed under arrest and taken to the city jail in the town business district. The policeman there is the same one you talked to before who advised you to ignore the "prank." You feel that this policeman is a reasonable and fairly unprejudiced individual, but that he is naive and really can't understand how you feel since he's never been in your shoes.

Policeman at the town business district: You are shocked when Coalhouse Walker, who talked to you previously about his predicament, is brought to your police station under arrest. You honestly didn't think the situation would escalate this far. When you read the official police report, you see that Coalhouse demanded an apology. You feel he's handled the situation badly and has pushed his luck by being too proud and arrogant.

STUDENT SAMPLE

"COALHOUSE AND THE POLICEMAN"

C: "Officer, would you tell me why I was arrested when I came to find justice."

P: "You were arrested because of being too proud, and also you pleaded so much."

C: "Well, actually I was trying to find my rights served to me and instead I was arrested." "I don't understand why is that wrong to beg for justice."

P: "It is sure right to talk about justice but it is not right to argue about it. Coalhouse we do know that a few people put dirt in your car and smashed you car, but still it is your own responsibility to find a way to move your car. It is not our responsibility. It is our job to arrest people who doesn't obey the rules, you disobeyed so we had to arrest you."

C: "In that case, are you saying that if I didn't argue with the officer I wouldn't be arrested right now, and instead I would get my car cleaned, and my custom fabric top replaced?"

P: "No, you couldn't get your car cleaned, but at least we would have helped you move the car. But you didn't listen to us, all you did was arguing."

C: "Well, if I couldn't get my car cleaned then why am I wasting my time with the officer I felt that I was mistreated because I am a black American, would you agree with me?"

P: "No, no one had mistreated you. We are talking about the rules and regulations. It was your own fault, because you didn't move your car (not even tried) and you argued about it. This is not a case of discrimination. We never discriminate against black people."

Activity 3

Dramatization

Rationale: This activity of "being" the character forces students to take on the thoughts and feelings of the person they are portraying. "Becoming" the character takes students one step beyond discussion questions, and forces them to search for an inner rationale for their characters' thoughts and actions.

Procedure: The situations for the silent dialogue activity can also provide the basis for a subsequent dramatization. Once students have finished writing their dialogues, they should be asked to enact them. A question and answer session should be built into this activity in which the performers remain in their roles and are asked to explain further their statements or actions to members of the student audience. Ideally, the entire activity (i.e., the enactment and the question-and-answer sessions) should be videotaped. The videotape of this activity can then be used to give students feedback on their oral performance, and to elicit further class discussion regarding the motivation and personality traits of the characters involved.

STUDENT SAMPLE

Bruno—manipulation   Coalhouse—confrontation

Once upon time Bruno Betleheim was seating in one of the New York's parks. One black man came up to him and ask, "What time is it?" Bruno Betleheim looked at his watch, and answered "It's 12:45." At this moment this man noticed some numbers on Bruno's hand.

C: What are those numbers on your hand?
B: Oh well, it's a long story. I was in concentration camp in Nazi Germany. I had no rights out there. I had an infaction on my hand, and I would of lose my hand. Prisoners couldn't get any medical treatment, unless it was related to work. The more a prisoner pleaded, the more annoyed and violent the SS private became. So I had to act temperate and not to show the pain. After I got my treatment, I began to walk. The guard called me back and gave me a card for the further treatment, which I didn't expect. Now I can to the country wher I can have any rights.
C: May be you right, but I didn't get any respect even from the police.
B: What's your name by the way?
C: My name is Coalhouse Walker. I was driving down the road and fire-team was blocking the way. When I asked to go off the road than they asked to pay a fee. I knew it was fake and decided to go to the police station. I didn't any help out there either. After I arrived to my car. It was off the road, it had whole in the roof, and a mound of human excrement.
B: Unbellievable, I can't understand. How come American police could do such things to the people.
C: You'll have to believe in it. I wanted to get my rights, and I got 15 years in jail. Even lawyers did not want to fight for me.
B: But why? They're guilty not you. There's nothing wrong that you did.
C: That's true. I was guilty just because I was black. And only now I can understand it. My own country was a concentration camp.

Activity 4

Analytical Essay

Rationale: The preceding activities should have enabled students to immerse themselves in both the language and the thematic dilemmas presented in the two passages. While the topics below are challenging, they are within the reach of high-intermediate limited English proficient students.

Procedure: Select from the analytical essay topics below, and assign one as an in-class or out-of-class essay topic. Multiple drafts of the essay should be encouraged.

Topic 1: Compare the attitudes and actions of the labor camp guard with those of the fire chief and his men. Among the points you might consider are their ideas about the people they're oppressing, their ways of showing their feelings, and their reactions to the behavior of Bruno Bettelheim and Coalhouse Walker.

Topic 2: Bruno Bettelheim was a prisoner in a labor camp, threatened with sickness and death; his aim in his encounter with the guard was simple survival. Coalhouse Walker, on the other hand, sought from fellow-citizens—and public officials—the equality he was guaranteed under the law. Analyze how their emotions and their strategies for dealing with mistreatment reflect their different aims.

Topic 3: In the essay from which the Bruno Bettelheim selection is taken, the author suggests that oppressed people can sometimes manipulate their oppressors into doing what they want. Do you agree? And do you approve of that manipulation instead of straight-forward resistance? Write a persuasive essay arguing your views on these questions, making specific reference to the Bettelheim and Walker passages.

STUDENT SAMPLE

The two passages, we read, bring us different aspects of discrimination. In one Bruno Bettelheim experienced discrimination as a prisoner in a Nazi labor camp. And Coalhouse Walker experienced discrimination as a black in the U.S. at the beginning of the century. One of the aspects is the difference between the attitudes and actions of each oppressor to the people he is oppressing.

The labor camp guard who was in charge of the clinic was very cruel, brutal man. When Bruno asked to have the dead flesh cut away, he started to pull at the festering skin. He felt contempt toward Jews and very superior. He remarked proudly that he could not be taken in by Jews . . ." He had a very clear stereotypes on Jews—they are submissive, weeping, servile, pleading persons, and most of all they try all the time to get more than they deserve. He declared that the time that Jews could react their goals by lamentations. The more prisoners pleaded, the more annoyed and violent he became, and stories at previous services rendered to Germany outraged him.

In Coalhouse Walker's story there are some similar tellings. The firemen also had very superior and disdainted to Walker. They block his way and then they insolt him demand a toll so they will have money for firetruck so they will be able to drive to fires just like he drives to whorehouses. Then when Walker demand his rights the Chief began to laugh. And the policeman advised him to go back to the car because the firemen were tired from the fun. The firemen tell they have the right to suppress Walker.

Bruno Bettelhiem contradicted the labor camp guards stereotyp on Jews. For the first time the guard come across such a strong brave prisoner. The conflict cause him to see Bettelheim differently and deal with him differently. Unlike the guard sterotyp on Jews Bruno is matter-of-fact, avoiding pleading deference or arrogance: he shows stronger and does not show signs of pain. And as soon as the cutting of the dead flesh was over he started to leave—Bruno didn't try to get anything more then he asked for in the begnning. The guard was so surprised that he decided to give him further treatment.

In Coalhouse Walker's case though he did contradicte the firemen views on black and he did stand for his rights, the firemen interpreted it as a joke. Coalhouse demand pay for the damage. The Chief began to laugh and his men come out to join the fun. As Walker still insisted they started to see this as insolence and even as a threat. As the policeman notice Coalhouse's dignified speech, his dress and the fact he is owning a car, he grew angry. They were amazed by his behavior but they saw it as a provocation, which caused them to treat Walker harder. The policeman decides to arrest him on false charges. I belive that the reasons for the difference in the behaviours of the camp guard and the firemen is the position in which Bettelheim and Walker were in. The jews in the War World II lacked any rights. They were just like a toy in the hands of the Germans. Bruno didn't demand anything, he didn't even think that he had something to ask for. He just tried to get through one more day. And that is what caused the guard to give him the treatment. Coalhouse belived that he has rights and he demand them. I think that the fact he did have those rights theoreticly made the firemen very uneasy and pushed them to treat him so badly.

SOME FINAL REMARKS

The simple presentation of a text does not guarantee understanding and enjoyment for language minority students. With their developing linguistic abilities and differing cultural frames of reference, these students can be intimidated initially by the many lexical, cultural, and stylistic hurdles in a text. But through carefully selected activities, students can recognize bits and pieces of themselves and their life experiences or knowledge bases in the ideas that they encounter in a given reading passage. With guidance they will be able to recognize these parallels, and through guided close reading they will find the evidence they need to to reason effectively and to support their arguments.

Our mandate as language and content teachers serving the language minority population is to make challenging texts accessible to these students, who bring eager minds to our classrooms but are limited in terms of the language skills which they possess. It is our mandate as well to infuse the curriculum with a fresh spirit—the spirit of analytical reading and writing. We cannot achieve these purposes without "hooking" students into text—that is, helping them see that even within the most challenging texts there are reflections of their own thoughts and experiences. In other words, we must guide the students into bringing their life experiences to bear in relating to the texts they read in all their courses.

The activities we have mapped out in this chapter all involve making text more visual, tangible, personal, and thereby accessible. We encourage you to experiment with these activities. Take what appeals to you and appears useful.

Adapt these activities to your own purposes and to the works that you have selected to teach. Good luck guiding your students on their journey!

NOTES

1. The *Into, Through,* and *Beyond* model was originally designed by members of the California Literature Project. We have taken certain liberties with this model, and adapted it for our own purposes—to assist language minority students in accessing challenging text. Many of the activities in this chapter are of our own design, though we freely acknowledge our debt to the originators of this model.

2. Language teachers interested in enriching their curriculum through literature should see Appendix B for a discussion of criteria for choosing accessible texts.

3. These passages and the analytical essay topics included in this chapter are from a version of the UCLA Writing Programs Placement Test for freshman students. Many thanks to George Gadda for his careful editing of these passages and for his permission to use these materials. The passages were initially selected by Robert Cullen, now of CSU San José.

4. The passages may not, in fact, be suitable for all students due to the sensitive nature of their central theme. Teachers who opt to use the passages should therefore consider their own students' experiences with prejudice and/or oppression before opting to use the unit in its intact form.

5. We are particularly grateful to Linda Rasmussen and Yoko Tice for the help they gave in constructing this unit. Many thanks are due as well to the other participants of the 1988/89 Teaching Analytical Reading and Writing Project, who gave us ideas for unit development.

BREAKING NEW GROUND: RESPONDING TO *LEP* WRITERS IN EVERY CLASSROOM

Faye Peitzman ■ *Beth Winningham*

> I like to do a lots of writings, because it helps me learn. I have a chance to practice to write English. It also helps me learn more because after the [lesson], I have to think about that, and write some sentences to you. Then, you will ask me back somethings, or teach me something by write on the papers. I feel it is interesting when we talk by writing. . . .
>
> Huong
> ESL/Life Science

As the benefits of writing-to-learn have become generally known, teachers across the disciplines have often felt torn between the need to "cover" sufficient subject content and the understanding that their students will acquire that content more fully if they write about it. While in the past five years growing numbers of history, science, literature, and math teachers have embraced journal writing, learning logs, short-answer questions and essay writing, many have yet to incorporate much writing into their curriculum.

Teachers of language minority students have been even less inclined to ask their students to write. Because sheltering techniques necessitate slowing down subject matter presentation anyway, the notion of carving out time for writing assignments seems problematic. In addition, teachers of language minority students often feel that writing is not their students' best way of demonstrating content mastery—so why choose a mode that may seem to frustrate and limit them? The fact is, however, that language minority students—like their native English-speaking peers—also learn in different and deeper ways when they put pen to paper. Further, these students clearly need frequent experiences in writing—both in ESL and in all content classes—if they are to become equal participants in mainstream classrooms.

Can students still in the process of acquiring English really benefit from writing across the disciplines? Will their teachers gain insights into how these students are "reading" class discussions and activities, as well as written texts? Will something even more powerful happen when teachers like Huong's "ask back" or teach by writing back? In this chapter, we invite you to join us in breaking new ground: weaving opportunities for students to write into the fabric of ongoing classroom activities and responding both to tentative journal entries and to more formal reports and essays.

In this chapter, we divide our suggestions for means of responding to students' work into two main categories, dependent upon classroom goals (see Figure 5.1). If their purpose is to enable students to rethink or expand upon subject matter concepts, teachers can engage students in interactive journals. If students are to have the opportunity to revise an entire paper, then teachers and student peer groups or partners can make suggestions for changes in content, and perhaps also in organization, style, diction, and mechanics. There may be yet a third purpose for responding to student work: if the purpose is for students to gain an overview of how they have developed over time as learners and/or writers, then both teachers and students review a portfolio of the students' work periodically and at the end of the term.[1]

IF THE PURPOSE IS FOR STUDENTS TO:	THEN:	AND:
1. Rethink/expand upon subject matter concepts	Teachers ask questions in students' journals and engage students in essay dialogues	Students clarify, specify, offer additional information in response to questions posed by their teacher
2. Revise entire essay	Teachers and peers ask questions and make comments that prompt changes in content, organization, diction, mechanics	Students consider the suggestions made by teachers and peers
3. Gain overview of how students have developed as learners/writers	Teachers review students' portfolios periodically and at the end of the term	Students review their own portfolios periodically and determine in what ways they've increased their understanding of content matter and/or grown as writers

Figure 5.1.   Response Models across the Disciplines

TEACHER QUESTIONING IN INTERACTIVE JOURNALS

Language proficiency, educational background, personal experience, and interest in the subject—these are just a few of the factors that account for the diversity of readiness and achievement within a single classroom. Interactive journals, journals that contain students' writing and teacher questions about that writing, can accommodate this great diversity because students will write at the level they are able, and teachers can adjust their questioning style to fit each student. Students and their teacher focus exclusively on subject matter issues. Language errors are not corrected, but teachers' written responses provide models of correct spelling, grammar, and syntax. The journals, then, provide an excellent opportunity for students to "talk aloud" on paper and for teachers to assume the role of coach rather than judge.

A few quick examples of this exchange. In each example, the student's journal entry is followed by the teacher's response. The first comes from Dario, a student in an ESL/American history class:

> Now I'm gonna talk about what a new immigrant should do when they come to a new country. Well you have two choices assimilate the new culture or maintain your own culture. For me I mean, for my own I chose to assimilate the majority culture because I'm living in this country but without forget my own culture.
>
> *How have you assimilated, Dario? In what ways have you changed and in what ways have you kept your first culture?*

This teacher's questions were designed to encourage Dario to be more specific in identifying the ways in which he has either assimilated or maintained his first culture. This additional information would demonstrate the extent to which Dario understood the concepts of "assimilation" and "culture."

In a biology lab, students observed what happened when ten sow bugs were placed in a petri dish divided into four sections. Each section represented a different environment: dry and light, dry and dark, wet and light, wet and dark. After students observed the experiment, they wrote in their journals what they saw and determined which environment the sow bug preferred.

> This lab had bugs called sow bugs and petri dish, paper and sand. We are seeing what environment the sow bug like best. First we put two kinds of sand that are wet and dry. Then we made half with a paper cover over it and the other side has light. We have four environments (different) for see what the bug likes to live.
>
> When we put the bugs inside the dish we wait to see where they will go. I think they like the dark side but I don't know. We wait and then I look and the bugs go to the dark and some are wet and some are dry.

I liked your prediction that the sow bugs will prefer the dark side. Why did you think that this would happen?

We waited only 10 minutes, didn't we? What do you think would happen if we waited a longer time, say overnight, to give the bugs a chance to move?

Carolina correctly observed that the bugs did not choose any one single environment in the ten minutes allotted to the experiment (a shorter time than was originally planned). However, because most of the students had previously seen sow bugs in their natural environment, Carolina's teacher encouraged her to draw on her background experience in order to make bolder predictions.

In a world history class, students were studying the contributions made by various cultures. They had recently read and discussed a textbook chapter describing the contributions and key components of Aztec society. The teacher asked students to write in their journals about what life might have been like in Aztec society. Aygun chose to personalize her answer by becoming an Aztec woman.

I am a Aztec woman. I lived in a big city named Tenochtitlan. We have many gods and they sometimes are angry gods. And they send me sun and rain and help me growing my crops. I have corn and other crops to grow and eat for my family.

I know what day it is because we have a calendar. Also we pray to the gods for help and we have special days and everybody goes to the place the people watch the priests give a ceremony.

What do you mean when you say "they sometimes are angry gods," Agyun? Can you give me an example?

Ceremony is an important part of Aztec life. I'm glad you mentioned it. Can you describe one type of ceremony and explain its purpose?

In this case the teacher had initially posed a very general question. She then asked the students to continue writing in their journals about the areas they seemed to be most interested in.

In an ESL pre-algebra class, one teacher uses dialogue journals to discover where a student may have stumbled when working on a problem. By asking her students to explain the process they went through to get an answer, this teacher helps her students understand the process of math and the importance of checking or rethinking their work. We can see that this student's shortcoming was merely a careless error in the mathematical operation of the problem:

"An unknown number decreased by 14.7 equals 20.3. Find the unknown number."

Let d = unknown number.

I will attempt this word problem by:

First—read the problem carefully.

Second—identify the variable, d = unknown number.

Third—Look for the key word, which in this problem is decreased. Which applies subtraction.

Fourth—Write the equation which is:

d – 14.7 = 20.3

Fifth—Solve the equation, and look for the variable.

Sixth—Adding the same number to each side of an equation forms an equivalent equation.

d – 14.7 + 14.7 = 20.3 + 14.7

Seventh—You add to solve for the variable.

d = 38.00

Eighth—You check the solution by substituting the variable for the number.

38.00 – 14.7 = 20.3

Ninth—If the equation is not balanced you go back and check the whole process again, but if it does balanced means you got it.

20.3 = 20.3

Tenth—The unknown number is 38.

I can see that you understand how to go about solving this kind of problem. How is it, though, that 20.3 + 14.7 = 38.0?

In another world history class, after listening to the song "We Shall Overcome" and discussing discrimination in society, students were asked to write about what our society has yet to overcome. Given that this was early in the year and that the topic was broad and relatively unstructured, their teacher announced that if students were having great difficulty expressing themselves in English, they could write in their first language—and she would do her best to get it translated.

A few students took advantage of this offer. While most teachers will not be able to offer students this freedom on a regular basis, the advantages of such a strategy are apparent in the following dialogue:

What shall we overcome? We shall over come to be more carelles to every body. And to do not descriminate people for what they are. Y todos tenemos que ayudarnos para que no se cometan injusticias sobre nosotros por ser latinos, ya que todas somos iguales. Aunque a varias personas no les guste.

How proud you should be to write in two languages! You are right that Latin people have suffered many injustices even today. Can you tell me what some of the injustices are and how we could overcome them?

The student replied to her teacher's questioning:

Some injustices are that many employers don't give a job to someone who don't speak english well even if that job don't need it. Also that the policies treat us like we are criminal went we make an error. Sush, went we drive without licence or if went we cross the street went the ligh is red. Also many white people call us (mojados) "wetbacks" even if we are not. Just because we look spanish.

For this student, it would seem that the teacher's positive attitude about having abilities in two languages and the teacher's willingness to make efforts to understand the student's first language have engendered trust and willingness to risk and to try harder to write in English. Compared to the first, the second effort shows promising signs of growth in fluency, level of correctness, and the writer's ability to express a point of view.

Interactive Journals in Life Science: A Case Study

When Henry Chau and Linda Sasser collaborated on shaping a journal component for his three-week ecology unit, they found that intermediate and advanced ESL students caught on immediately and that students and teacher benefited greatly. Among the results:

- Teacher and students established a new kind of personal connection.
- The teacher could see just how well students were understanding the class lectures and discussions.
- The teacher had the opportunity to push students' critical thinking forward.
- Students received individualized attention.
- Students who were not used to admitting they didn't understand became less reticent about asking for help.

The classroom procedures were simple. The last 15 minutes of class three days a week were reserved for journal writing—in this case, answering a question that followed naturally from the classwork of the day or previous few days. Students would turn in their journals at the end of the class period; journals would be returned in two days' time with a response from the teacher.

Over the three-week period, students wrote to the following questions:

1. Do you think ecology is an important subject? Why?
2. Can the earth run out of energy as we run out of money? (This alludes to a classroom example.)
3. Can we feed more people with meat or vegetables? Why?
4. If you are a fish farmer and you own the pond, what will you do? (This refers indirectly to an example given in class.)
5. How would you feel if you lived in this town and worked for the company? (This refers to a case study read in class.)
6. Write down the reasons why the world is at risk.
7. What are some possible solutions? (to the world's being at risk)
8. What is it like to be living in a polluted city?

While these questions did require general comprehension of class lectures, discussions and some readings, they almost always went beyond direct recall of information presented in them. Rather, they were phrased to see if students could use the information presented to come to new insights and understandings. And if students didn't demonstrate understanding the first time around, the teacher's response could always probe for it in a slightly different way.

The following are excerpts from the dialogue journal of Esteban, one of the more skilled writers in this ESL/Life Science class, and a student who understood immediately what it meant to keep up his end of the correspondence.

> Can the earth run out of energy as we run out of money? I don't think the earth can run out of energy like we run out of money. Because if we run out of money we can find it back but if the earth doesn't have energy then a lot of organism will die and nothing can survive.

> *This is a grim conclusion (and one I agree with). So, how can we make sure that the earth will have enough energy to last for ten million more years?*

> I'm not sure. What do you mean by saying how can we keep the energy for the earth.

> *The earth's energy comes from the sun, the oceans, the plants, and the animals. We can't control what happens to the sun, but we can affect the other energy sources. What happens if the oceans become polluted, or we use all the trees for firewood and houses, or eat all the animals?*

> If we use all the trees for firewood and eat all the animals and the ocean become polluted then I think that the earth would turn out to be a desert. The earth becomes beautiful and livingful depend on these three things. So if we destroy all these then we will be disappear from earth either.

Esteban would keep at it as long as the teacher would—and in fact this dialogue did continue with an additional entry by each. Most of the other students couldn't quite keep this pace (in each writing session they had only fifteen minutes both to respond to teacher questions about past entries and to write the new one.) And many students were straining to understand the concepts presented. Sometimes they missed the point of the question posed. For example, Huong tries his best with the third question, "Can we feed more people with meat or vegetables?"

> It is depend on people what they like to eat. If people like to eat vegetables, then it is good for their body. And if people like to eat meat, then it's make yur body has more energy. So, both vegetables and meats are the tonic food for your body.
>
> *Good nutritional sense! But, if you had 1,000,000 people to feed, which source of food would feed them more efficiently? Meat or vegetables?*
>
> Meat is better.

In this case, the dialogue let the teacher know that Huong had not yet internalized the presention on the energy pyramid and, if a good number of his peers had similar problems, perhaps it should be reviewed with the class. In the next entry, though, Huong at first neglects to consider an important factor but later demonstrates that he did understand the dilemma of a fish farmer who was losing his fish to a snapping turtle:

> 'If you are a fish farmer and you own the pond, what will you do?' I will feed all fishes in the pond every day. My responsibiity is to give them feed three times a day. Sometimes I will put some fresh vegetables in the pond, too. I also have to take care of them every day, that's mean i have to keep the pond clean, and never let children go down there, or never let animals fall down. Sometimes, if the fishes are sick, then I will call a doctor, and put them in the separate pond, until they get well. If some fishes are grow bigger, then i can sell them to the market. This is my own business. I like it because all fishes look beautiful to me, and adorable. This is what I will do, if I were a fish farmer.
>
> *You are a thrifty and careful aquaculturist. But, if I were a turtle, I would love being in your pond—there would be so many delicious fish to eat!*
>
> If there is a turtle in the pond, then I will take it out. Then I try to make other pond, and take care it just as I feed my fishes.

Thao also wasn't clear what to do with this question. He takes a significant risk in his initial response, telling the teacher that he does not understand. This provokes an extended dialogue:

> I'm not sure I understand the question.

Okay—let me draw the question: Is this clearer? Now, what will you do?

I think I should take out the one hungry turtle and put into the ocean. So it wouldn't eat the fish. I will feed the fish and every day go out and see how the fish is doing. See if the fish need anything.

Could the turtle live in salt-water? What kind of "anything" might your fish need?

The kind of "anything" might my fish need are enough oxygen, food and have clean water.

Toward the end of the unit, Thao offered a thoughtful response to the question of offering possible solutions to a world at risk:

There are some possible solutins that can save the world from danger. I think strong laws are needed to stop companies from dump toxic wastes. For example, the government should write a letter to the companies tell them not to dump toxic wastes if they not listen, closed it down. Stop cut down trees.

Don't you agree that we already have strong laws? Union Carbide was guilty of poisoning the people of Bopal, India and Exxon was found guilty of polluting Prince Edward Sound in Alaska. Yet both companies are still in business. Would heavier punishment make the big companies more careful?

I'm not sure about heavier punishment make the big companies more careful because the light punishment didn't do anything to stop this company. How heavier punishment make them to stop. Wait a little awhile and see what the companies going to do to harm the pollution. If they did, I think the government should break up the companies.

As in all classes, in this sheltered life-science class there was a range of current ability levels, both in science and in English. According to the students, the interactive journal could accommodate them all:

- This writing process can help me to review all the things in class and I can give my opinion to someone too. It helps me by letting me some new idea. (Esteban)

- I really enjoy writing things that I have learned to you. It does help me alot in understanding more about the lessons that I learned because every time I write out what I learned, it helps me to remember it. Also, sometimes I understand something but I can't express it. Thus, if I still have a chance to write like this and have someone to read, like you're doing right now, I think I'll improve my writing as well as understanding the lessons. However, I need a lot of time to express my ideas, too—at least 15 minutes. (Hue)

- I like this kind the work because it help me to understand more beside just write the note. Before my grade was very low and always lazy to do the work, but now I like to work more. . . . I learn many things. It was more easy to understand and write the important things. . . . I glad the test was not too hard for me and that test, I was the first time gave that high. It was 7 1/2 and I feel very happy because I did listen for the subject. I don't have to memory a lot. (Maggie)

- I think it is a kind of funny for me to write this project because it can make me know more about life science, its can make me create new interesting idea, and it also can make my mind work well on it. . . . So may be it will become easy for me. I also hope that I could be a scientist on someday. (Laura)

Commenting on Drafts

So far our primary focus has been on writing to learn, assisting students to master concepts and facts in the various disciplines. In the process of our students' writing and responding to our questions about their writing, they develop as learners in specific disciplines and—as a bonus—also expand their repertoire as writers.

In this section, we keep that dual focus of helping students grow as learners of the content areas and as critical thinkers. Now, however, we place more emphasis on how teachers can help limited English proficient students move toward the fluency, form, and correctness that characterize the writing of the most skilled of their native English-speaking peers. One of the essential keys to growth in LEP writers is the continued opportunity to draft, revise, and receive comments from teachers—and also from peers—on how they might make their papers stronger: more insightful, better organized, more fully developed, easier to read, more consistently correct. We have found that the following guidelines for commenting on drafts, adapted from guidelines for teachers of native English-speaking students, meet many of the needs of teachers of language minority writers when they take major writing assignments in the content areas through more than one draft.

The first version of these guidelines was developed in 1982 when a group of thirty-seven UCLA lecturers and high school English teachers reviewed the research on the theory and practice of responding to student writing, shared their own best strategies, and, from there, agreed on both a philosophy and practical guide for writing comments that would be of use to students as they revised. In 1987, a smaller group of UCLA faculty and high school ESL teachers made additions to these guidelines to meet some of the challenges teachers of limited English proficient writers face. (See Gadda, Peitzman, and Walsh, eds., 1988.) The guidelines in Figure 5.2 are further tailored to meet the needs of teachers across the disciplines. Why these particular guidelines? Our rationale is as follows:

We *skim the student's draft and read "over"*—that is, ignore—*sentence-level errors to get a sense of the whole.* We thus avoid writing comments early on that we no longer want to say by the time we've finished reading the full paper. We have found that it is indeed possible to read "over" the many errors that may characterize writing of LEP students.

We *praise major strengths* because students learn at least as much from understanding the power of their successes as they do from learning about the problems yet to be tackled. At times, parts of students' own papers can serve as

---

- Skim the entire draft before writing comments. Read "over" sentence-level errors.

- Praise major strengths or students' efforts.

- Question students' ideas that are

  — promising, but not fully developed,

  — unclear to you because of students' limited English proficiency,

  — clearly erroneous interpretations or presentations of fact.

- Treat cases of plagiarism with sensitivity.

- Do not feel responsible for direct error correction. Paraphrase parts of the students' texts when students need a model for precise vocabulary, sentence structure, or spelling. Feel assured that your written response will help students with issues of content and language.

- Be supportive in tone throughout.

Figure 5.2. Guidelines for Commenting on Drafts across the Disciplines

models to guide the rewriting of weaker sections. There will also be times when teachers won't be able to identify real strengths. At these times teachers can *acknowledge any honest effort* that went into the student's attempt.

We have found that *"text-specific" questioning* is an invaluable technique for helping students revise. Rather than writing in the margin "be clear!"—which is a difficult command to act on if the writing was clear to the writer to begin with—we ask specific questions rooted in the student's own text. By answering these questions, students end up clarifying for themselves and their readers the problematic parts of their texts.

We *treat cases of plagiarism with sensitivity* because often when LEP writers copy phrases, sentences, and even paragraphs from another text, they are not trying to deceive the teacher about what is their own work. Rather, it may be that they are able to understand the text but not ready to use their own words to explain it. They may not have the confidence to paraphrase. Also, they may have been taught in their home country that it is not only acceptable to copy but evidence of strong scholarship to "know" the words of authorities. Our dual responsibility is to teach students that plagiarism is not acceptable in our schools and to give students guidance on how to "let go" of the safety they feel in copying others' texts.

Content teachers should *not feel responsible for direct error correction*. A particularly good strategy that bypasses direct error correcting but achieves the same results—students have models of correct English—is to paraphrase a small part of the student's text. When teachers are able to understand the sentences they paraphrase, they may decide to say, "I agree with you that. . ." When they aren't sure of the student's meaning, they may pose a brief follow-up question. This kind of individual attention, which offers students help with issues of content and language simultaneously, has the potential to make dramatic impact on students' achievement in content area and on development of writing abilities. It is also an invaluable assistance to the ESL and English composition teacher.

Finally, a *supportive tone* may carry more weight than our most astute observations. When students know that the teacher is on their side, they will take the risks necessary to promote growth in thinking and writing. An anthology of comments that address many issues important to the writing of LEP students while maintaining a supportive tone can be found in Appendix C.

COMMENTS ON REPORTS WRITTEN IN ESL LIFE SCIENCE

The impetus for one writing project in which limited English proficient students in an ESL life-science class drafted and revised reports of two to three pages from a field trip to the San Diego Zoo. All the students demonstrated great interest in the excursion and fascination with the animals. Their teacher wanted to capitalize on this excitement and to help his students see that they could find information in places other than their class textbooks—and that they had the ability to organize their own reports and use their own words. Thus, students were assigned to write a report on an animal of their choice after consulting one or two books. The teacher stressed that the report had to have an introduction that let the reader know why the student chose the animal and that stated the topics to be discussed in the body of the paper. The conclusion was to be a summary which briefly reiterated particularly interesting facts.

In the report entitled "Bats," Bonnie, a native speaker of Chinese, was able to demonstrate both personal engagement with her topic and a fine attempt at learning from other texts.

BATS

① There are several reasons why I would like to choose bats for my science project. They always give me a chilling feelings because they always appear at night. Most of the horrible movies have bats in the haunted house. Therefore, I would like to learn more about the actual bats. I'm going to introduce about the myth, the breeding activity, echolocation, and migration.

Bats are the only mammals that can fly. There is a Chinese mythology talked about why bats smiliar like human but looks like a bird. Once upon a time, there was a temple in China. The door was always open and bats praid in the temple all the time. They hoped to change to human beging. Then they got to change their teeth, hair, and face to men and the rest of their body still remain birdlike. After that they were too shame to go out at day time, so they only leave the temple at night time. In day time they keep praying and hope they can return to birds. In Chinese bat is also a symbol of good luck and long life. Many of the emperor and emperess liked to bat's design for decrorations.

② Talking about bats breeding habits. Most of them have only one or two babys per year. Different species have different patterns. For example, Big Brown Bats from North America usually have twins. Bats always give birth in late spring, May or June in the northern hemisphere, November and December in the southern hemisphere. In winter the spermatozoa will store in the uterus of the female, and the testes of the male shrink as sperm production ceases. During the winter in the hibernating species the egg follicle in the ovary slowly enlarges, while the vagina becames filled by a plug formed from the mucous secretion of its walls. When spring arrives and the bats again come into regular activity, this plug is cast, ovulation takes place, and the egg starts down the oviduct, into which meanwhile the spermatozoa have made their way, and thus fertilization is effected by means of the stored sperm.

③ One of the special ability that bats have which give them a privilege to live in darkness. Many scientists wanted to find out how counld they do that. They do many experiments. One of the Italian scientist in the late 1700's, Lazarro Spallanzani, inserted brass tubes into a bat's ears, it could orient only when the tubes were open, if he blocked the tubes the bat would fly helplessly.

Biologists reconized that some bats seem to move seasonally from place to place in a predictable pattern. Mexican Free-tailed Bats spent their summer at the south-western United States and parts of Mexico. They travel almost 1,300 kilometres to Mexico in winter. There are large number of insects in Mexico which provide the bats a lot of food supply in winter. The Common Bent-winged Bats live in Australia in summer and travel to Europe when Australia turns cold.

④ I am glad to introduce the real facts and stories about bats here. I think there are still a lot of interesting facts about for us to find out. In my spare time, I will find out more about them.

Bonnie chose these animals because of the "chilling feelings" they give her, particularly when she thinks of them in their usual pop culture habitat—haunted houses. The paragraph concerning myths of bats in the Chinese culture suggests that she is relating her own cultural background to the world of the academic classroom. The rest of the paper is straightforward in its approach and, with the exception of a few lines about the breeding of bats, seems to be in her own words. A comment to Bonnie offers praise and pushes for an even stronger draft.

Dear Bonnie,

Congratulations on writing an organized and thoughtful research paper on bats. You accomplished a great deal by including a myth about bats and the factual information that scientific research is able to tell us.

In your revision, see if you can add more of your own words in your third paragraph and use some examples in the conclusion.

1. This is a strong opening paragraph because you state what you plan to do very clearly.
2. This paragraph begins fine, but with the sentence beginning "In the winter . . ." can you change these sentences into your own words and emphasize the important information about the breeding habits of the bat?
3. Is this "special ability" called echolocation, a word you mention in the first paragraph?
4. For your summary, could you give some examples of the "real" facts about bats? Did learning these facts change the "chilling feelings" you wrote about in paragraph 1?

You've done a nice job, Bonnie, and I look forward to your final report.

—B.W.

Mario, another student in the class, chose to write about turtles. With the exception of his introduction, he has very obviously copied from one book. Why? The level of language command evident in the section labeled "Introduction" gives part of the answer: Mario is clearly struggling with the written form of the English language. The other part may simply be that he is inexperienced with writing reports in any language. What follows is Mario's introduction and the first paragraph of the body of his paper.

INTRODUCTION

And this introduction we have all about the turtle. that introduction show. HWo the turtle. Enveloped over Earth.

Like they can traveler from afar.

Also How they leaving the sea behind. Also we have to know if the turtle is a reptile. the turtle is an animal smart, that they find their own place for the nest.

Also. we find digging out the nest. and explained all about the Eggs. disguising the nest. laying more eggs. and How the baby turtle Hatch out. everything. How the little turtles growing up. and How the turtles rush to the sea: what Kind the dangerous. the have to pass. and some interesting facts about the turtle.

THE TURTLE

Travelers from Afar

It is moonlit night. Crowds of green turtles are coming out of the sea onto the beaches of Ascension Island. With the help of their powerful flippers they have swum 1,240 miles from their grounds around the coast of Brazil. They have come to lay their eggs on this island in the Atlantic Ocean. The places where they lay them are called spawning grounds.

The rest of the typed four pages is organized under the following captions: "Leaving the Sea Behind," "The Turtle As Reptile," "A Place for the Nest," "Digging Out the Nest," "The Eggs," "Disguising the Nest," "Laying More Eggs," "The Baby Turtles Hatch Out," "The Rush to the Sea," "Some Interesting Facts about Turtles." The written comment that follows notes what the student has accomplished, reminds him that the class was asked to begin their papers by stating *why* they chose the particular animal, focuses on the need to put the report in his own words, and—most importantly—offers some help in achieving that goal.

Dear Mario,

I know you prepared this report with great care. Your illustrations and detailed report tell me that turtles really interest you. What I'd like you to do in your introduction is to explain <u>why</u> turtles fascinate you so much.

Now let's look at the typed parts of your paper. In a research paper, the writer needs to use his own words to describe his subject. You have many good ideas, but you need to pick out the important ones and explain them in your paper the best way you can.

When I read your paper, I see that you talk about three important subjects about turtles:

1. What the turtle looks like
2. Where the turtle lives
3. How the turtle reproduces

Can you go back to your paper and organize it into three different parts, one for each subject? Then, you can look at your notes in order to remember what information you want to include, but use your own words, Mario.

I will be interested to learn what you think about turtles in your revision.

—B.W.

The teacher who wrote to Mario recognized that his extensive copying was not an attempt to cheat but rather a first step toward presenting information from a text. The suggestion for revising the introduction lets him know that his feelings about the topic are important. The suggestion to reorganize will push him to take more control of how he composes his information.

COMMENTS ON WRITING ABOUT LITERATURE

Next, we discuss two essays about literature written by junior high students followed by teacher comments written to help them revise. The students had read and discussed a passage from Richard Wright's *Black Boy* that is sometimes anthologized under the title, "Hunger." In five pages Wright tells the story of a young boy—perhaps seven years old—who learns what hunger feels like after his father deserts the family. When his mother finds work outside the house, young Richard is given the job of doing the grocery shopping. On his first shopping trip, he encounters a gang of boys who knock him down and steal his money. His mother sends him out again, and the gang repeats its actions. When Richard returns to his home sobbing, his mother listens to his story but won't let him enter the safety of his home. She gives him more money: "Take this money, this note, and this stick," she says. When Richard tries to elude her and slip into the house, she slaps him and promises to whip him if he comes into the house without the groceries. That night the boy Richard wins "the right to the streets of Memphis."

Several junior high classes of ESL 2–4 students spent one week with their teacher listening to the passage being read aloud, reading sections of it in collaborative groups, discussing key vocabulary, and talking about the issues the passage suggested. Then, they had one class period to write to the following prompt:

> Why does Richard's mother send him into the streets to buy groceries a third time? Do you think her actions were good for Richard? Feel free to draw on your own experiences in developing your essay.

The following two essays represent the upper and lower range of the writing these students produced in a one-hour period. We selected Ricky's piece because it demonstrates very perceptive thinking even though there are errors in every sentence, and in at least one case the intended meaning is totally obscure to an outside reader. Roberto's we included because the reading and writing task was still somewhat beyond his reach. Yet he, too, is a member of the class and can be helped to develop as a writer. Here, then, are the two essays, the comments written to each writer, and the rationale for the comments made:

RICHARD'S TOUGH TIMES
by Ricky

① ②   The reseaons that I think his mother send him out the next time is because she want him to know how the street or lift it about, when you are poor. My other reason the his mother send him out to buy groceries. It because she want him to fight and not be ③ afair of anybody. Maybe it that his mother need food. My best reason that I could think of is the she work so hard and had to stand up to her husband living with no money. If she could take that feel so could Richard and the he had to do alot of thing by himself and not to be told. May be that Richard mother is upset and taking all of her feel to Richard.

I'm not sure because Richard mother have her right and wrong. Her right is that she must tell Richard to talk care of him self and his family when his father is not here. She probably think that Richard is big now and must now how to take care of him self on the street. Her wrong if that her push him to much and he think that he is not able to do it. Or the Richard's mother is harm if on Richard because his father left the But at the end her mother told him how to stand up to people when they poor and lived in a bad neighborhood.

④   My experiences of developing is when I was 12. I hard that my god father was dead. I was suprise. I felt like something inside of me was gone and gone forever. It told me a long time to amited to my self that my godfather had past away. But my father told me

that what ever is gone is gone and told me to stand up to it. My
⑤ experiences-developing it like Richard Mother. But she took it harder
than I did, she took her feeling all on Richard.

My other experiences was that I was afair to go to the doctor,
My mother always forces me to see the dinsite. By at the end was
happy that I went to see the dinsite, when my teeth is loose.

Comment to Ricky

Ricky,

It was a pleasure for me to read your paper. You really made a valiant
attempt to get inside the head and heart of Richard's mother. Good for you!

When you revise, I'd like you to focus on the very beginning and ending
of your paper.

1. Pretend your reader isn't very familiar with the reading passage. Can
   you help your reader by mentioning the author and title of the reading
   in your opening?

2. I'm not sure what you mean when you write "She want him to know
   how the street or lift it about." Can you say this in other words?

3. Your "best reason" is a perceptive one. Richard's mother has been
   under a lot of stress. Maybe she is, in part, taking her feelings out on
   Richard.

4. I know you're answering the second part of the question, but pretend
   the reader doesn't know the question and explain what you are doing.

5. Can you describe a little more in what way this experience was similar
   and different to Richard's? That would make a good ending for your
   paper—perhaps you don't need the dentist example.

I'm sure your revision will be very fine!

—FP

Ricky's insights into the feelings an adult might have were quite impressive;
most thirteen- and fourteen-year-olds chose to label the mother a cruel person.
The first and fourth comments try to teach Ricky the conventions of essay
writing as opposed to simply answering test questions. The second numbered

comment focuses on the only line in the paper that was truly unintelligible. It is quite likely that Ricky knows what he meant and will indeed be able to say this in other words. Comment three offers well-deserved recognition of perceptive thinking. Further, the paraphrasing/summarizing serves to give Ricky vocabulary he may want to adopt in his next draft: being under stress, taking feelings out on someone. In the last sentence of paragraph three Ricky attempts to fulfill the demands of the prompt—"draw on your own experiences." He offers experiences but doesn't explicitly let the reader know their connection to the first two paragraphs. The comment also suggests that the dentist example be dropped. Ricky could choose, however, to expand on this example and make it work.

UNTITLED
by Roberto

① So Richard's can fight fore his writes. And be barde and cacas.
② But if Richard's didn't go he was going to be witer by his morther and if he didn't fight but Richard's went in and won the fights. And
③ came home with his groceries.

④ It theng so.

Comment to Roberto

Roberto,

"Hunger" was a difficult reading. I can tell that you have understood it. Your next job is to revise your answers to the questions.

1. You have given a good answer here. Richard's mother sends him into the street so he can fight for his rights. She is helping him to become brave and courageous.
2. You are also correct here. If Richard didn't fight for his rights, his mother would have whipped him.
3. Though Richard's mother forced him to be brave, he did fight. He won the fight and came home with the groceries.
4. Please tell me more! You say that you think the mother's actions were good for Richard. I agree! In your revision, tell me why you think this.

I am very interested in reading your next draft.

—LS

Deciding how to respond to Roberto's paper was somewhat more difficult. At first glance there doesn't seem to be anything to praise. Roberto obviously did, however, understand the gist of the story and did attempt to answer the two questions posed. The first three numbered comments are paraphrases and expansions of Roberto's words and ideas. He will be able to draw on their spelling, vocabulary, and sentence structure when he writes his next draft. Roberto's "It theng so" was a direct response to the second question in the prompt. It's up to him now to give reasons. After open class discussions that are yet to come, he should be able to generate his own response. The final note offers interest in what Roberto will compose for his next draft.

PRACTICAL AND PHILOSOPHICAL ISSUES

Teacher Time

Of course, these written comments are just one part of what teachers do to help student writers. After Ricky's teacher discovers that most of her students have had no experience in distinguishing between answering test questions and writing a short essay, she may make the conventions of the essay the focus of some of her brief "mini-lessons." When the class understands that they are to assume the reader doesn't know the precise question asked and that they need to set up an introduction and provide transitions between paragraphs, then a three-minute version of the comment to Ricky might serve just as well.

Three-Minute Comment to Ricky

Ricky,

Great attempt to get inside the head and heart of Richard's mother—especially where I've placed an asterisk in the margin. When you revise:

1. Can you rephrase? Just what does Richard's mother want him to know how to do?
2. Can you say more about how your experience was similar to and different from Richard's? That would make a fine ending.

—FP

As the shortened comment to Ricky illustrates, teacher comments may be brief and not particularly time-consuming. What is most important is that they convey the voice of a reader who is rooting for the students' success and who offers particular questions that the students should consider. In addition, after teachers have modeled how to offer helpful responses, pairs of students can respond to each other.

Students' Roles in Commenting

Clearly peer response serves to help teachers with the burden of the paper load. Equally important, it enables students to have a more active and responsible role in their own learning. While LEP students will not be experts on editing issues, they are able to state what they think is significant or strong in a piece of writing and to ask questions that help their peers develop their ideas more fully.

In addition, students and teachers both benefit when students have a role in guiding the way their teachers read and comment on their drafts. When students are asked to write a cover letter that specifies the kind of help they particularly want, they gain a greater awareness of themselves as writers and feel more ownership of their work. Teachers learn where students feel they need help and thus can offer it more purposefully.

The two letters that follow were written by community college ESL writers who were drafting research papers:

My research question: Is there a logical explanation for all the supernatural phenomenon going on the burmuda triangle?

First I gave my thesis question and answer, then cited some incidents happened in the triangle. I listed down all possible answers that scientist have theorized which is the main content of my paper then draw on my conclusion.

I had a good time doing this paper but the only problem I encountered was there was a lot of things to be put in a short paper. I hope you can help me edit some parts of it to make it shorter and please tell me if I have presented my report clearly and arrange it correctly.

Thank you very much!!!

—Victor

I chose the subject regarding a comtemporary political issue: British colony Hong Kong is going to be returned to China in 1997. Alone with that, there are lot of happiness, sadness, satisfaction, unsatisfaction, involved, as well as political argue, aproval or disproval this big event among the world wide range especially to the chinese people overseas and Hong Kong neative people. What I try to find out is the tipical views among them which represents the feeling of those people towards this extraordinary change.

As to my Article, the part I'm pretty satisfied is the whole process of interview. I had almost every advantage to get a good one which I did as matter on fact. Please focus on my gramatic errors and especially spelling mistakes.

—Yue

In the process of writing the letters, the students inevitably gain awareness of their learning/composing process. Their teacher can make sure to address their stated concerns—though she certainly isn't limited to focusing exclusively on them, particularly in the case of Yue, who only seems to want a proofreader. Yue's letter does bring up an important issue, however. How do we respond to students who ask us for direct correction of error?

Issues of Correctness: For ESL and English Teachers—Mostly

Our goal is to enable all limited English proficient students to attain the written fluency and correctness of our most talented mainstream students. The question becomes when and how to intervene, as well as <u>who</u> should intervene. Ideally, all teachers care about their students' writing, but in reality only the ESL teacher may have time to help students with grammar systematically. And subject matter teachers must not be deflected from assigning writing from a fear of dealing with the "correctness" problem.

This is not a recommendation for any teacher to correct all errors for students. Recall the written response to Roberto on page 108. In it, the teacher comment focused on content but provided a model for correctness—giving correct spelling and grammatical structures. How would Roberto have felt if he received the response in Figure 5.3 instead?

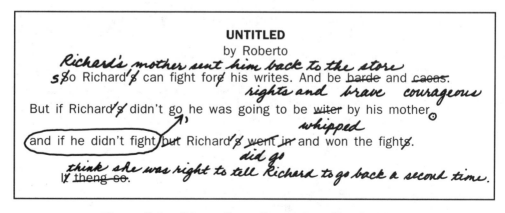

Figure 5.3. Direct Error Correction: The Problem

Here every error has been dutifully corrected, fragments have been expanded to sentences, a phrase has even been reordered. A student at Roberto's stage of language acquisition would almost certainly be overwhelmed by the markings and would be reduced to simply recopying for the next draft. In addition, it's unlikely Roberto would understand all the corrections in a way that would permit transfer of knowledge to editing another paper. In cases like this, indirect correction of error—such as the paraphrasing embedded in the teacher comment on page 108 is more appropriate. Other strategies that help students acquire standard English forms include old-fashioned copying—which enables students to internalize language: its spelling, usage, and sentence structure—and dictation and stylistic imitation.[2]

If over-attention to form impedes beginning writers of English, total lack of attention to the errors of more advanced students—adolescents who have reached intermediate fluency—is clearly problematic. (Recall the statements of some of the case-study students interviewed in Chapter 1.) These students have already "picked up" impressive skills from their experiences in sheltered classrooms and from a great deal of exposure to print. Still, almost all will need instruction that directly focuses on their particular needs. For these students who are developmentally ready—and particularly for the ones who ask us for help—what can we do? Here are some strategies that have proved successful:

- Identify patterns of errors or egregious errors and select two or three types to point out—either by correcting them or underlining them for students to correct. Students can keep a log of these error types and edit for them in future papers.

- Pair students after they have received their drafts back and ask them to work together in correcting the errors on both of the papers. The opportunity to "talk out" the reasons for the changes can be particularly valuable.

- Ask students to read their papers aloud to each other. Often simply hearing the language out loud will be sufficient to help them begin the self-editing process.

- Select a small section of a long paper and, on a tape recorder, talk out reactions and suggestions for revision. Often it is not possible to do word-by-word "corrections" that leave students with a model of good writing. And sometimes there are alternate ways of solving stylistic revision problems. Particularly when time for conferencing during class is limited, students benefit from hearing their teacher's speech which includes the very idioms, use of articles, and precise turns of phrase that they are ready to acquire.

- Use the overhead for whole class instruction on common problems. Students benefit greatly from a nonthreatening demonstration of selected error correction on papers that are not their own.

FINAL THOUGHTS

Most of this chapter has focused on the power of writing to learn—an important opportunity for limited English proficient students. This is perhaps one of those "uncommon sense" notions that John Mayher talks about in his book by the same name. Indeed, the commonsense premise would be that LEP students couldn't possibly learn content through writing. Instead, we have seen that as content teachers are breaking new ground by incorporating writing into their sheltered classrooms, students are indeed growing in both language abilities and content mastery. We hope that the different perspective provided in this chapter serves as an invitation for all teachers to engage their students in dialogues across the disciplines.

NOTES

1. Portfolio assessment is beyond the scope of this chapter. For helpful discussions of portfolio assessment, see J. Mumme (1990); S. Murphy and M. A. Smith (1990); and D. Wolf (1989).
2. For more extensive suggestions for helping students to acquire standard English grammar and to increase their stylistic repertoire, see J. Frodesen (1991); M. Shaughnessy (1977); and P. Taylor, ed. (1989).

WHAT'S FAIR? ASSESSING SUBJECT MATTER KNOWLEDGE OF LEP STUDENTS IN SHELTERED CLASSROOMS

Dan Fichtner ■ *Faye Peitzman* ■ *Linda Sasser*

> In my country I was always a top student. But here I get Cs and Ds because of my English. I am so angry because I know I haven't changed. I'm still smart. But my teachers, they think I'm stupid.
>
> Leticia

Chances are that Leticia's teachers don't think she's stupid. More likely, they are grappling with a variety of philosophical and practical issues linked to assessing the knowledge that limited English proficient students have gained in sheltered content courses. Indeed, in the interrelated realm of assessment and evaluation, pain and confusion characterize the reactions of teachers as well as students. Many of the recurring concerns of the teachers we spoke with center around testing modes, language issues, and grading:

- Can multiple-choice, machine-scored tests adequately evaluate language minority students? They often give up and mark at random.
- I'm stuck with multiple-choice and true-false tests because when my students write, I don't know how to separate their ideas from their spelling and grammar.
- How do I construct assessment activities that let LEP students demonstrate all they know about my subject?
- How do I grade without discouraging the students with grades that might be too low and then over-encouraging with grades that are too high?

Part of the dilemma in assessing LEP students' achievement is that in order for sheltered classrooms to work optimally, the students should be at an intermediate fluency level of English production. This can be seen at a glance in Figure 6.1. Further, traditional assessment formats that at first might seem to work in favor of students who are not proficient in producing language themselves—such as multiple choice and fill-in-the-blank—are actually quite

Level of English Production	Student Characteristics	Learning Strategies in English	Appropriate mode of delivery for content
Preproduction	Receptive Silent period Environment enhances ability to comprehend Receptive vocabulary: @ 500 words	Responding to instructions & commands Nonverbal demonstration of comprehension Pointing, gesturing, drawing	Primary language
Early production	Receptive Very limited production, one and two word phrases Environment enhances ability to comprehend Receptive vocabulary: @ 1000 words Productive vocabulary: @ 100 words	Nonverbal demonstration of comprehension Yes/no answers One/two-word answers Listing, sorting, categorizing	Primary language
Speech emergence	Limited production Expanding rapidly Longer strings of language Ability to dialogue Ability to sustain a narrative Receptive vocabulary: @ 2,500–5,000 words Productive vocabulary: @ 250–500 words	Questioning Longer answers (phrases) Open-ended exchanges Emerging literacy in English	Primary language
Intermediate fluency	Understand almost all speech directed to them Produce connected narrative Ability to interact extensively w/native speakers	Reading/writing comprehension Development of CALP in English Still need comprehensible input Vocabulary development needed	Sheltered English

Derived from S. Krashen and T. Terrell, (1983), *The Natural Approach.*

Figure 6.1. Relationship of English Proficiency Levels to Content-Area Instruction

language-intensive, requiring students to read very carefully and discriminatingly. The use of distractors, negatives, and quantifiers in such tests often serves to confuse rather than enable students.

The demanding time limits that characterize most assessment procedures are also problematic. For most limited English proficient students, beat-the-clock testing engenders much anxiety and puts students in a high-risk situation. Time constraints in short-answer and essay tests cause LEP students to make more errors than usual, with the result that even experienced teachers may have trouble understanding their students' responses. Time constraints coupled with reading demands in multiple-choice tests may well cause students to "give up and mark at random." Representative student comments on matters of assessment are very telling. The comments in Figure 6.2 demonstrate LEP

True/False

Words are tricky. In English there's many words which mean the same thing, but they're written in different way.

Oh, I hate that! Like, which one is NOT true. I get so confuse.

True/False is good if students have to write the answer to correct the false sentences.

Fill-in-the-Blank

I don't like because sometimes it's hard to know what is the right word to put in.

I never get a good grade on this even if I study.

I can not figure the words. The only ways I can do if the teacher gives the whole list for us before the test day.

It's always tricky test because if I thought it would a noun but sometime is an adjective or a verb.

Multiple Choice

In US History I'd studied hard and the teacher give us multiple choice test. I studied very hard but he wanted to know what is the best answer. I got very confuse and my grade was low.

I never had multiple choice test before I came here. I just had short questions and answers, those kind.

Short Answer

I might not like short answer, but it's a really good way for test because it can test out whether the student had understood or not.

This kind is harder because I have to remember the complete answer and know a lot about certain questions. But is easy when the teacher give me an idea what is going be about the test.

This is okay for a test, but some teachers ask too many questions. There's no time to finish. Three or five questions would be fine.

A question like "give me the function of mitosis" is too general. When I take the test and he goes over the answer, he says, "that's right but is not what I wanted." How could I know what he wants?

Figure 6.2. Student Views on Forms of Testing

students' passionate desire to demonstrate what they know; they also anticipate some of the adjustments in assessment strategies that sheltered classroom teachers across the disciplines have found promising.

What's fair? Or what's left? Our goal in this chapter is to focus on the kinds of adjustments to commonly used assessment techniques that enable students to demonstrate the extent of their understanding of subject-matter facts and concepts. The theme that will run through the following examples and discussions all point to the importance of teachers' flexibility in their approach to assessment and to an expanded repertoire of assessment techniques that can be drawn upon. Of course, all instructional activities, such as those described in Chapters 2, 4, and 5, can also serve as evaluation tools. Most of our examples will center on ways teachers have begun to modify and expand short-answer and essay assessments. As the university students in Chapter 1 remind us, ultimately our LEP students will have to demonstrate what they know through writing; helping them gain the proficiency to do so remains our goal. In the meantime, however, we will consider ways to assess content knowledge that take into account our students' developing mastery of academic English.

MODIFYING AND EXPANDING TRADITIONAL ASSESSMENTS

> I am very hated writing because sometime I cannot do very well for it and it is hard for me.
>
> Sam

In Chapter 5, the authors propose that inviting limited English proficient students to write is essential in advancing both content knowledge and language ability. Writing is both an opportunity to demonstrate learning and a chance to learn further by elaborating, analyzing, and synthesizing. At the same time, paper-and-pencil assignments and tests often fall short of revealing what LEP students understand in their content courses. What we need to do, then, is pair writing components with additional avenues—less language-dependent—so that students continue to have the chance to shape what they know and learn through the process. We also need to ensure that students have sufficient time to accomplish their tasks. How can we create enabling environments for assessing our students? The following guidelines underlie the more specific examples of assessment that follow.

Minimize the demands of processing the task. Teacher observations and student reports suggest that limited English proficient students will typically take three times as long as native English-speaking peers to read written texts. When teachers read test directions aloud to students in addition to providing them in written form, processing demands are minimized. Ideally, teachers will check that students understand what they are supposed to do.

Encourage graphic illustrations to accompany written answers. LEP students are often very creative in demonstrating their understanding through pictures, charts, and graphic organizers. Graphic organizers allow students to demonstrate a great deal of knowledge in a relatively short amount of time. They may also serve to help students compose short essays.

Vary the number of test items and/or modes of representing understanding for students at various levels of English proficiency. Although officially they shouldn't, some sheltered classrooms will contain students below the level of intermediate fluency. When teachers ask more proficient students to answer four questions, they should consider allowing less proficient students to answer one and jot down notes for the others. These students may also be able to communicate their understanding orally or visually.

Minimize the element of surprise and number of tasks in end-of-year tests. Collaboration between teacher and class in developing possible final test questions has multiple benefits. Allowing students to prepare outlines outside of class for use on test day enables demonstration of both range and depth of understanding.

Intervene in the assessment process. Performance testing offers opportunities for teachers to redirect students so that one "misreading" early on doesn't preclude students from getting back on track. More traditional assessment procedures can also make room for teacher intervention. For example, if students' written responses fail to clarify whether or not they have comprehended test questions and/or course material, teachers can ask them to answer some of these questions orally.

GRAPHICS SHOWING COMPREHENSION AND LEADING TO SHORT ESSAYS

Even students at the early production level of English proficiency will be able to demonstrate understanding of key concepts by drawing diagrams or illustrations. For example, in Figure 6.3, a student in a sheltered history class has successfully described in picture form the process of bartering—the exchange of goods without the use of money.

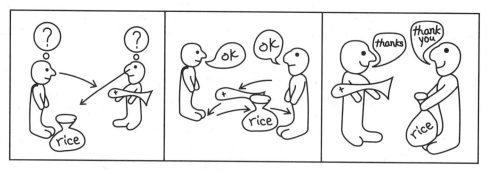

Figure 6.3.   Barter

Figure 6.4 shows one student's short answer essay with pictorial support that explains the sequence of events leading to the formation of hail. The illustration itself demonstrates understanding, and students continue with written descriptions to the extent they are able.

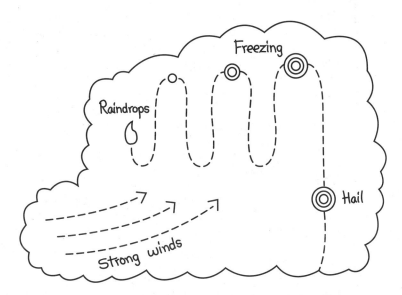

First it is a raindrop it drops and the strong wind blow them up back. Second it freezes and then it goes down again. Third the wind blows the raindrops up again. Fourth the raindrops freezes and fell down again, next the wind blows it up again. Five it freezes and it gets larger, then it fells down again in form of hail.

Figure 6.4. Sequence of Events of Hail

Students may also be asked to use graphic organizers as a prewriting strategy. After studying the causes of the Civil War, students listed advantages for the North and the South. Using the T-graph format that the teacher drew on the board as a model, students filled in their answers and then wrote a brief essay (Figure 6.5). The T-graph enabled students to organize what they knew; that preliminary step then allowed them to ease their way into writing a short-answer response about which advantages were most important to the conduct of the war.

Figure 6.6 illustrates another way graphic organizers can be used to help students demonstrate knowledge and begin to write short answer essay

Civil War Advantages	
North	South
larger population	got support from England at first
more factories	
	good trained generals (more)
more ability to make the military weapons, warship, etc.	the war was fought in its own territory.
lots of horses and mules	
good railroad network	The strategy of the South was only to defend
large supply of goods	

From the personal point of view, I think to hold the war fought on the South's own territory was the most important advantage for the South and in the Civil War. There are some reasons for this. First, fighting on their own land, the troops in the South don't have to get food or military supplies from far away. They could get these supplies more easily than the North. Second, fighting on their own land, the strategy of the South only had to consider to defend the attack from the North. They don't have to use too many soldiers and sent them to far away to attack the North. Third, the soldiers in the South would know the land shape, the geography better and adjusted the weather condition in their own homeland. The above show that how important and advantages if the war happened in people's own territory.

Figure 6.5. T-Graph: Student Sample

questions. All students in a history class were asked to fill in the charts with phrases explaining the "who," "what," "where," "why," and "how" of three important historical phenomena of the 1930s and 1940s. These charts were used to assess their understanding and knowledge of the terms *Great Depression, Invasion,* and *Dictator.* Because this sheltered class contained students with a large range of language abilities, their teacher offered alternative tasks to students at the various proficiency levels. Some students explained the chart in a paragraph, and students who had reached intermediate fluency tackled a longer essay on the Great Depression. In such assessments, the key is to ask students to do something at the upper end of their ability range.

	Great Depression	Invasion	Dictator
Who		Germ + Austria, Poland, Czecho.	Hitler-Germany Mussolini-Italy a powerful leader
What	many had no jobs	go into	
Where	all over the world		
When	1930's		1930's
Why	speculation on stocks "crash of 1929"	to get factoers and raw material	G.D.-promised food, jobs and "greatness"
How		took over the countries by force	
Importance Connection	one of the reasons for WWII		started WWII

Great Depression

The Great Depression happened in 1930's because of the speculation in stocks—"Crash of 1929". It concerned all over the world. Many people had lost jobs. It is important because it is one of the reasons connections for World War II.

Dictator

Dictators who were powerful leaders appeared in 1930's. Two of the dictators were Hitler in Germany and Mussolini in Italy. Appearance of dictators made World War II.

Figure 6.6. Matrix and Short Answer: Student Sample

ESSAY EXAMS—REMOVING THE ELEMENT OF SURPRISE

Students who have reached intermediate fluency in English should be asked to write essays about course content. They will not be successful, however, if there are unrealistic time limits, if written directions come to them cold and unclarified by oral elaborations, or if the questions are not a logical result of the work studied in class. The questions themselves, however, can certainly be rigorous, demanding analysis and synthesis. Consider this final exam in a sheltered U.S. history class:

1. Jefferson and Hamilton did not agree on many of the issues facing the new nation after the ratification of the new constitution. What was the basis for their disagreements, and what were at least three of the areas of disagreement? Explain the stands of each on the issues.

2. Localism has been a problem for the United States ever since its earliest beginnings. Define "localism" and show how it manifested in at least three different periods that we have studied. Does localism exist today? Are there any examples? Is localism good or bad?

3. The United States increased in size greatly during the early and middle 1800s. Different methods were used to obtain this growth. Define "Manifest Destiny," and describe at least three different ways in which the United States followed this policy. Is this policy possible today? Why or why not?

4. We have met many interesting characters in the first 200 or so years of U.S. history that we have already studied. Choose one of them and give a brief biographical sketch of the person, being sure to include why the person is famous. Include at the end of the essay three or four questions that you would ask the person if he or she were alive today.

To create an enabling assessment environment, this teacher modified the usual way of administering an essay exam. First, the topics were generated by both the teacher and students in a class discussion: all reviewed the year's work and decided which topics were really of importance. Students and teacher clustered on the blackboard the various topics; later, the teacher shaped those topics into four essay questions. Students were asked to take home the sheet of final topics and cluster or outline their responses to the questions at home. They were permitted to use their text and classroom notes. On the day of the test, they submitted their outlines; their teacher reviewed these outlines while they took the objective part of the test. Then they rolled a die to determine which of the four questions they would write out in class. The students had prepared all four, but wrote only one, thus defeating their demon—time.

GRADING OUR STUDENTS, ASSESSING OUR ASSESSMENTS

I strongly believe that it's a teacher's responsibility to make sure that the grades aren't a main concern of their students, but encourage them to learn the materials rather than panicking the night before a test.

Anthony

I think the teacher should be more understanding about grading a student. If she sees that the student is trying hard to get good grades, if by any chance he gets a D she should give him a C since she knows he's trying. But at the test he just couldn't do it because sometimes you get nervous on tests and you forget how to say in English.

Rosa

In an ideal world, students and teacher would not be so preoccupied with grades. As Anthony suggests, understanding and knowledge should be our focal point, not grades. The reality, however, is that grades are important and students' motivation and feelings of self-worth are often very much ruled by them.

None of us wants to fail a limited English proficient student who is obviously putting in great effort. Giving a C for effort alone is problematic; students need to demonstrate that they have acquired course content, just as their native English-speaking peers do. Giving grades of "credit/noncredit" until students perform at C level would be ideal, except that many universities require letter grades for the course to count toward subject requirements. Some districts have devised a system whereby students who receive a D repeat the course but do not fail. This preserves self-esteem to some extent.

These issues, though, may well be resolved as we continue to develop assessment strategies that do enable students to demonstrate the extent of their understanding. As we continue to look with different eyes at our students and at ways of assessing their growth, we'll succeed in finding out what's fair.

APPENDIX A: PASSAGES ABOUT BRUNO BETTELHEIM AND COALHOUSE WALKER

PASSAGE ONE

> Explanatory Note: In 1938, Bruno Bettelheim, a Jewish psychologist, was a prisoner in a Nazi labor camp. He suffered a severe case of frostbite, but medical help was only provided for work-related accidents, and prisoners who sought help for any other problems—like frostbite—were often abused. Eventually Bettelheim risked visiting the clinic. He tells the following story.

No Jewish prisoner ahead of me in the line was admitted to the clinic. The more a prisoner pleaded, the more annoyed and violent the SS private became. Expressions of pain amused him; stories of previous services rendered to Germany outraged him. He proudly remarked that he could not be taken in by Jews, and fortunately the time had passed when Jews could reach their goals by lamentations.

When my turn came, he asked me in a screeching voice if I knew that work accidents were the only reason for admitting Jews to the clinic, and if I came because of such an accident. I replied that I knew the rules, but that I couldn't work unless my hands were freed of the dead flesh. Since prisoners were not allowed to have knives, I asked to have the dead flesh cut away. I tried to be matter-of-fact, avoiding pleading, deference, or arrogance. He replied: "If that's all you want, I'll tear the flesh off myself." And he started to pull at the festering skin. Because it did not come off as easily as he may have expected, or for some other reason, he waved me into the clinic.

Inside, he gave me an angry look and pushed me into the treatment room. There he told the prisoner orderly to attend to the wound. While this was being done, the guard watched me closely for signs of pain, but I was able to suppress them. As soon as the cutting was over, I started to leave. The guard showed surprise and asked why I didn't wait for further treatment. I said I had gotten the service I had asked for, at which he told the orderly to make an exception and treat my hand. After I had left the room, he called me back and gave me a card entitling me to further treatment, and admittance to the clinic without inspection at the entrance.

PASSAGE TWO

Explanatory Note: Coalhouse Walker is a central character in E. L. Doctorow's *Ragtime*, a novel set in and around New York City at the beginning of this century. Walker is a successful black musician. What follows is a condensation of a key scene in the novel, in which Walker attempts to drive his custom Model T Ford through a small suburb back into New York City.

Coalhouse Walker's trip back to New York took him past a company of volunteer firemen. Whenever he passed the fire station in the past, the firemen would fall silent and stare at him. He was aware that in his dress and as the owner of a car he was a provocation to many white people. All his life he had coped with such feelings.

As the black man drove along, a team of three horses pulled a fire engine into the road ahead of him and stopped, blocking the road. The firemen advised Walker that he could not drive on without paying a $25 toll. "This is a public thoroughfare," Walker said, "I've traveled it dozens of times and no one has ever said anything about a toll."

Walker decided to back up and go another way. At this moment, however, several firemen carried out ladders and other equipment, all of which they set down behind Walker's car. The Fire Chief explained to Walker that while the toll had never been collected, it was nevertheless in force. "We need the money for a fire truck," he explained, "so we can drive to fires just like you drive to whorehouses."

Coalhouse calmly considered the courses of action available to him. Apparently it did not occur to him to ingratiate himself. Instead he asked two black teenagers to watch his car and then walked back toward the town's business district. A policeman there advised Walker to go back to his car: "They don't mean no harm. They're most likely tired of the fun by now." Walker may have realized that this was probably the maximum support he could expect from a policeman, and he wondered if he was perhaps oversensitive to what was really just a prank. So he went back.

His car stood off the road in a field. It was spattered with mud. There was a six-inch tear in the custom fabric top. Deposited in the back seat was a mound of human excrement. Coalhouse confronted the Chief, who now agreed that there was no toll. Walker said he wanted his car cleaned and the damage paid for. The Chief began to laugh, and a couple of his men came out to join the fun.

At this moment a police van drove up, carrying two officers. They talked to the Fire Chief, who explained that the car had to be moved since it was blocking the station. The larger policeman took Coalhouse aside. "Listen," he said. "We'll push your car back on the road and you be on your way. There's no real damage done."

"I was on my way when they stopped me," Coalhouse said. "They put filth in my car and tore a hole in the top. I want the car cleaned and the damage paid for." The officer had now begun to notice Coalhouse's dignified speech, his dress, and the phenomenon of his owning a car in the first place. The officer grew angry. "If you don't get out of here," he said loudly, "I'm going to charge you with driving off the road, drunkenness, and making an unsightly nuisance."

"I do not drink," Coalhouse said. "I did not drive my car off the road nor slash the roof. I want the damage paid for, and I want an apology." The policeman looked at the Fire Chief, who was grinning. He said to Coalhouse, "I'm placing you under arrest. You'll come with me."

APPENDIX B: SELECTING LITERATURE FOR LANGUAGE MINORITY STUDENTS

Literature for the school curriculum should "give insight, nourishment, [and] genuine mental and emotional pleasure" (California Literature Institute, 1985, p. 192). Such works, however, need not necessarily belong to the realms of the "great books." Rather, assuming that the works have intrinsic merit, and are not trivial, they can include works of lesser-known authors as well as those of better-known literary figures. The guidelines below, which summarize the background literature on the topic, are intended to help teachers on the local level select literary works for use in the ESL classroom:

- *Literary Value:* Above all, literature chosen for limited English proficient students should have emotional, intellectual, and aesthetic substance (California State Board of Education, 1985; Collie and Slater, 1987). In other words, the work should not be written solely for the purpose of entertainment; it should inform and engage students.

- *Interest:* Equally important is that the works of literature be able to stimulate personal involvement, that is, arouse students' interest and provoke personal reactions (Povey, 1979; Collie and Slater, 1987).

- *Relevance:* An oft-cited criterion for selecting literature is that the work should deal with themes of a universal nature (Stern, 1985). However, when selecting literature for language minority students, it is also important that students be able to "see themselves, their problems, and their culture reflected" (California Literature Institute, 1985, p. 192) or that the work reflect the geography and social conventions of the target culture (Povey, 1979; Robson, 1989).

- *Straightforwardness:* Clearly, works of literature selected for second-language learners need to exhibit a relative simplicity of linguistic and stylistic features, since otherwise, students' reading skills will be too taxed for them to enjoy the work in question. In this domain, it is suggested that works using nonstandard dialect, archaic vocabulary, and overly "literary" stylistic devices be avoided (Stern, 1985; Collie and Slater, 1987; Brown, 1988). Similarly, extended passages of "philosophising, description, or irrelevant dialogue may get in the way of the students' understanding" (Hill, 1986, p. 16).

- *Suitability:* The suitability of a literary work will obviously depend on the age and proficiency level of students as well as on their personal needs and interests. At lower levels of age and proficiency, whether a work is a "good read" (Hill, 1986) in terms of character and plot may function as the primary selection criterion. More mature readers will be more able to appreciate works for their intrinsic literary value, especially if the relevance factors mentioned above are taken into account.

- *Timeliness:* There is almost unanimous agreement that second-language students interact most successfully with contemporary literary works, that is, those employing modern-day language and set in the present time or not too recent past (Stern, 1985; Brown, 1988; Maley and Duff, 1989). Such "efficient and emulable contemporary prose" (Povey, 1979, p. 174) provides a rich source of input for students, which, if well chosen, is at a level slightly above students' comprehension level and can help to encourage language acquisition.

- *Brevity:* The relative importance of brevity in a literary work decreases in importance as the age and proficiency level of the students increase (California Literature Institute, 1985). Nonetheless, the length of the work remains an important factor, since students' limited reading skills in their second language will affect their ability to process longer texts. Thus short stories, essays, poems, and extracts from longer works are more usable in the context of literature-based language classes than are novels and plays used in their entirety.

- *Variety:* In terms of preparing language minority students for the analytical reading and writing demands which they will encounter at the university, it is important to "tap the wealth of literature in all genres" (California Literature Institute, 1985).

- *Appeal to the Teacher:* Lastly, the work should appeal to the teacher as well, since teachers will otherwise not be able to generate the necessary enthusiasm to teach a given work of literature (Povey, 1979). This suggests that the power to select literature for the school curriculum should be at the local rather than district levels, or that if the district mandates certain works of literature, that teachers at least be given choices from within this mandated literature.

Several questions logically arise in connection with the above criteria. What types of literature best meet these criteria? Do certain of the criteria receive heavier weighting than others in the decision-making process? What about literature in translation, "local" literature (i.e., Nigerian English), or simplified literature? And, finally, what about organizing the literature curriculum, and the sequencing of works within this curriculum?

There is no one simple or clear-cut answer to the above questions since classroom experience rather than empirical studies inform most of our decisions in this realm. However, at the risk of oversimplifying the issues, we can state the following. First, although the linguistic, cultural, and stylistic difficulties certainly serve as barriers to a work's comprehension by second-language readers, these alone are not adequate reasons for deciding against its use. Instead, the motivation of the reader to comprehend and interact is more significant, and thus the appeal and relevance of a work appears to be a higher order criterion than its linguistic, cultural, and stylistic "straightforwardness" (Collie and Slater, 1987).

Further, in terms of which works to select, audience considerations (i.e., what the age and proficiency level of students, and what their needs/interests are) and the syllabus parameters (i.e., whether the class focus is on language acquisition or literature appreciation) will certainly affect decisions of this nature. In EFL classes taught in contexts where English is a major language of communication (e.g., Kenya, Malaysia, India), teachers may experience a great deal of success using literature written in English by local authors, since students will be easily able to relate to the themes raised in such works; in ESL classes with homogeneous immigrant student populations, works written by members of that ethnic minority in English are likely to capture student interest; in literature-appreciation classes, teachers may wish to place heavier weight on the use of the well-known authors and classical works than in classes where literature is being used as the medium for the study of language; in classes where students are at beginning levels of proficiency but are mature intellectually, teachers may wish to use simplified literary texts; in classes where culture is the focus, lexical and stylistic considerations may take a back seat to the richness of cultural information in a given text.

In connection with the current interest in theme-based language teaching, there has been a trend toward organizing literature-based language curricula around certain themes or topics of general interest (California State Board of Education, 1985). Povey (1979) cites the example of a literature unit centered around the American cultural attitude toward the aged—one certain to occasion a reaction on the part of immigrants to this country. While we have no evidence that this approach toward organizing the literature curriculum is superior to others (i.e., a curriculum organized along genre lines, or one organized chronologically by literary period), this method of organization has strong inherent appeal, and certainly allows the teacher flexibility in integrating or "weaving" the various literary genres into coherent classroom units. Suffice to say, then, that with careful attention paid to selecting literature to meet the needs/interests of its intended audience and with adequate attention paid "up front" to preparing students to interact with the work (as discussed in Chapter 2), it is our strong belief that a literature-based curriculum can and will attain its goal of developing students' analytical reading and writing skills.

Donna Brinton
UCLA

APPENDIX C: SAMPLE COMMENTS FOR PROBLEMS OFTEN FOUND IN THE ANALYTICAL WRITING OF LANGUAGE MINORITY STUDENTS

Problems	Sample Comment
1. Global A. Plagiarism	Very often, especially toward the end, I find you rely heavily on phrases and even whole sentences from the passage. Be extremely careful about doing this, even when you are struggling hard to write well in English. You must show all borrowed language by enclosing it in quotes: "It was a gesture of deference and promise of filial submission." This is a very important point to keep in mind. When you rewrite, try to express your own ideas in your own words. Try not to rely too heavily on the words from the texts. Read the passages, think about what they mean, then write down your own ideas. See where I have marked 5, then look for other places on your own.
B. Organization	A strong introduction to a paper is very important. You mention some points in your introduction that you do not discuss in the rest of your essay. Your essay does discuss three strong points: matchmakers, gifts and showing respect. Your introduction should include these ideas. Paragraphs 2, 3, 6, and 7 all have strong topic sentences that tell me, the reader, where your ideas are going in each paragraph. Try looking at these paragraphs and then write topic sentences for paragraphs 4 and 5.
C. Support	These paragraphs have a clear focus and you've used good examples for support. Good job! I'd like you to reconsider the section in which you write where the celebrations take place. Is this an important difference between the two cultures, or an unimportant one? If it is not that important, I think you can leave it out. If it is important, then tell why you think so.

You might want to include the role of the mother-in-law in this paragraph. The reading tells us it is an important part of the Chinese wedding.

Perhaps your personal experience enables you to understand and describe the Chinese wedding in detail, but you also need examples from the Italian reading. Also, is your main point that both Chinese and Italian wedding celebrations are very elaborate? If so, let your reader know in a clear introductory statement.

D. Focus
(Point of view, central insight)

As you work on your revision, I would like you to think about clearly refocusing your ideas. For instance, reread the last line of the prompt. Do you have a central insight that unifies the entire essay? Try asking yourself questions like, "Are the customs mostly similar or different?" "How do the roles of women compare in the two cultures?" "Is marriage in the two cultures mostly between the man and the wife or between families?" The answers could give you your central insight. Then, you could build your introductory and concluding paragraphs on that insight.

This is a good introduction. In your conclusion, you state that the two cultures have some things in common. I think this is true. Can you also include this idea in the introduction? It gives the reader a clearer understanding.

(Tone or purpose)

I find your autobiographical comments delightful, but they are really out of place in an essay like this.

These are interesting comments about the kind of girl you wish to marry. However, they do not belong in an essay of this type. Stick to discussing what is contained in the essay.

E. Misreadings

Martha, I would like to suggest that you reread the passages and make sure what you write can be supported by the text. For example, you said that in both cultures the bride and the bridegroom didn't meet until the wedding day. Where does it say this? Did the matchmaker in the Chinese culture break off negotiations or the parents? See other 3s for more examples.

Reread the passage on the Italian wedding. The author says that it is NOT a romantic gesture. I think this paragraph has some untrue information. Can you check the passages again to be sure?

2. Sentence-Level
   A. Sentence Structure

This sentence is a run-on because it has two verbs, but you didn't use any punctuation to connect them. You will need to fix this sentence and look for other 3s to show you more.

In this paragraph, you have a lot of sentences that begin "He" or "She" and then a verb. These sentences make the paragraph sound choppy when it is read. Could you rewrite your sentences to show a little variety?

   B. Lexical Choice

Your attempt at vocabulary development is admirable but causes you to make mistakes in word usage. See other 4s in the margin and underlined words for examples.

Sometimes a dictionary will not give you the word you want to use. It is better to use vocabulary you are familiar with than to use your dictionary and pick the wrong word.

Once in a while you have chosen a word incorrectly (a look-alike or sound-alike of another word) or used a word in an unclear way. Look where I have marked 5s.

Here are places where you let the language of the readings take over and run away with you. To control this, try to state the facts and ideas you are using from the readings in your own words.

   C. Mechanics

When you have more time, check to see how some of the words you used are spelled. It might be difficult for a reader to understand what you mean if he is not sure which word you wanted to use.

   D. Word Form

Remember that nouns, adjectives, verbs, and adverbs all have different forms and have to be used correctly. See other 3s for words you need to change to their correct forms.

   E. Endings
      a. Plurals

When you forget to put the plural ending of a word (usually -s, -es, ies), the reader can't tell if you are referring to one or both of the cultures. See all the 4s for examples of places where you missed the plural endings.

      b. -s, -ed verb-form endings

Several times throughout your paper you dropped the -ed or -d ending on passive verbs. Even in the present tense, they need this ending.

I'm sure that given time you can correct these errors in subject/verb agreement. Look at your sentence, "The gifts is usually the jewelry and the money. The verb should be "are." Look for more of these kinds of errors or ask your teacher for help.

2. Articles

In a number of places, you have confused "the" with "a." If a noun is used for the first time, we usually use "a." Then it can be referred to as "the" after that point.

Reproduced from D. Brinton, L. Sasser, and B. Winningham. "The Limited English Proficient Student." In *Teaching Analytical Writing*, 1988, ed. G. Gadda, F. Peitzman, and W. Walsh, pp. 128–131.

REFERENCES

Bobrow, J. (1985). *Cliffs math review for standardized tests.* Lincoln, NE: Cliffs Notes.

Brinton, D., Sasser, L., and Winningham, B. (1988). The limited English proficient student. In G. Gadda, F. Peitzman, and W. Walsh (eds.), *Teaching analytical writing.* Los Angeles, CA: California Academic Partnership Program.

Brown, D. S. (1988). *A world of books: An annotated reading list for ESL/EFL students.* Second edition. Washington DC: TESOL.

Brown, H. D. (1987). *Principles of language learning and teaching.* Second edition. Englewood Cliffs, NJ: Prentice Hall.

California Literature Institute. (1985). *Literature for all students: A sourcebook for teachers.* Sacramento, CA: California State Department of Education.

California State Board of Education. (1985). *Model curriculum standards—grades nine through twelve: English/Language Arts.* Sacramento, CA: California State Department of Education.

Clark, W. V. T. (1940). *The oxbow incident.* New York: The New American Library.

Collie, J. and Slater, S. (1987). *Literature in the language classroom: A resource book of ideas and activities.* Cambridge, England: Cambridge University Press.

Connor, U. and Kaplan, R. B. (eds.). (1987). *Writing across languages: Analysis of L2 text.* Reading, MA: Addison-Wesley.

Crandall, J., Dale, T. C., Cuevas, G. J., Kessler, C., Quinn, M. E., King, M., Fagan, B., Bratt, T. and Baer, R. (1987). *ESL through content-area instruction: Mathematics, science, social studies.* Englewood Cliffs, NJ: Prentice Hall Regents.

Crandall, J., Dale, T. C., Rhodes, N. C., and Spanos, G. 1987. *English skills for algebra: Math-language activities for algebra students* [student text]. Englewood Cliffs, NJ: Prentice Hall Regents.

Cummins, J. (1981). The role of primary language development in promoting educational success for language minority students. In California Office of Bilingual Bicultural Education, *Schooling and language minority students: A theoretical framework.* Sacramento, CA: California State Department of Education.

Cummins, J. (1989). *Empowering minority students.* Sacramento, CA: California Association for Bilingual Education.

Frodesen, J. (1991). Grammar in writing. In M. Celce-Murcia (ed.), *Teaching English as a second or foreign language.* Second edition. New York: Newbury House.

Fathman, A. K. and Quinn, M. E. (1989). *Science for language learners* [student text]. Englewood Cliffs, NJ: Prentice Hall Regents.

Gadda, G. and Peitzman, F. (1984). Evaluation techniques. In J. Simmons (ed.), *The shortest distance to learning: A guidebook to writing across the curriculum.* Los Angeles, CA: University of California, Los Angeles, Center for Academic Interinstitutional Programs.

Gadda, G., Peitzman, F. and Walsh, W., eds. (1988). *Teaching analytical writing.* Los Angeles, CA: California Academic Partnership Program.

Gadda, G. and Walsh, W. (1988). Analytical writing in the university. In G. Gadda, F. Peitzman and W. Walsh (eds.), *Teaching analytical writing.* Los Angeles, CA: California Academic Partnership Program.

Heath, S. B. (1982). What no bedtime story means: Narrative skills at home and school. *Language in Society,* II (2), 49–76.

Heath, S. B. (1983). *Ways with words: Language, life, and work in communities and classrooms.* Cambridge, England: Cambridge University Press.

Heath, S. B. (1986). Sociocultural contexts of language development. In *Beyond language: Social and cultural factors in schooling language minority students.* Los Angeles, CA: Evaluation, Dissemination and Assessment Center, California State University, Los Angeles.

Heimlich, J. E. and Pittelman, S. D. (1986). *Semantic mapping: Classroom applications.* Newark, DE: International Reading Association.

Hill, J. (1986). *Using literature in language teaching.* London: Macmillan.

Horowitz, D. (1986). What professors actually require: Academic tasks for the ESL classroom. *TESOL Quarterly,* 20, 445–462.

Indrasuta, C. (1988). Narrative styles in the writing of Thai and American students. In A. C. Purves (ed.), *Writing across languages and cultures: Issues in contrastive rhetoric.* Beverly Hills, CA: Sage Publications.

Kaplan, R. B. (1966). Cultural thought patterns in intercultural education. *Language Learning,* 16, 1–20.

Kaplan, R. B. (1988). Contrastive rhetoric and second language learning: Notes toward a theory of contrastive rhetoric. In A. C. Purves (ed.), *Writing across languages and cultures: Issues in contrastive rhetoric.* Beverly Hills, CA: Sage Publications.

Krashen, S. and Terrell, D. (1983). *The natural approach: Language aquisition in the classroom.* Oxford: Pergamon Press.

Laosa, L. M. (1977). Socialization, education and continuity: The importance of the sociocultural context. *Young Children,* 21–27.

Levine, M. G. (1990). Sheltering U.S. history for limited English proficient students. *Social Studies Review,* 30, 27–39.

Maley, A. and Duff, A. (1989). The inward ear: Poetry in the language classroom. Cambridge University Press.

Matalene, C. (1985). Contrastive rhetoric: An American writing teacher in China. *College English,* 47, 789–808.

Mayher, J. S. (1990). *Uncommon sense: Theoretical practice in language education.* Portsmouth, NH: Heinemann.

McLaughlin, B. (1987). *Theories of second-language learning.* London: Edward Arnold.

Mumme, J. (1990). *Portfolio assessment in mathematics.* Santa Barbara, CA: California Mathematics Project.

Murphy, S. and Smith, M. A. (1990). Talking about portfolios. *The Quarterly of the National Writing Project and the Center for the Study of Writing,* 12 (2), 1–2, 24–27.

Naiman, N., Frohlich, M., Stern, H. H. and Todesco, A. (1978). The good language learner. *Research in education Series 7.* Toronto: Ontario Institute for Studies in Education.

Northcutt, L. and Watson, D. (1986). *S.E.T. sheltered English teaching handbook.* San Marcos, CA: AM Graphics and Printing.

Ostler, S. E. (1987). English in parallels: A comparison of English and Arabic prose. In V. Connor and R. B. Kaplan (eds.), *Writing across languages: Analysis of L2 text.* Reading, MA: Addison-Wesley.

Office of Budget, Institutional Planning and Analysis. (1989). *UCLA Fact Book 1989.* Los Angeles, CA: University of California, Los Angeles.

Peitzman, F. and Shideler, S. (1988). Commenting on student drafts: The teacher's role. In G. Gadda, F. Peitzman and W. Walsh (eds.), *Teaching analytical writing.* Los Angeles, CA: California Academic Partnership Program.

Politzer, R. L. and McGroarty, M. (1985). An exploratory study of learning behaviors and their relationship to gains in linguistic and communicative competence. *TESOL Quarterly,* 19 (1), 103–123.

Povey, J. (1979). The teaching of literature in advanced ESL classes. In M. Celce-Murcia and L. McIntosh (eds.), *Teaching English as a second or foreign language.* Rowley, MA: Newbury House.

Purves, A. C. (ed.). (1988). *Writing across languages and cultures: Issues in contrastive rhetoric.* Beverly Hills, CA: Sage Publications.

Reid, J. M. (1987). The learning style preferences of ESL students. *TESOL Quarterly,* 21 (1), 87–101.

Robson, A. C. (1989). The use of literature in ESL and culture-learning courses in U.S. colleges. *TESOL Newsletter,* 23 (4), 15–27.

Rubin, J. (1975). What the "good language learner" can teach us. *TESOL Quarterly,* 9 (1), 41–51.

Schifini, A. (1985). *Sheltered English: Content area instruction for limited English proficient students.* Los Angeles, CA: Los Angeles County Office of Education.

Schumann, J. H. (1986). Research on the acculturation model for second language acquisition. *Journal of Multilingual and Multicultural Development,* 7 (5), 379–392.

Shaughnessy, M. (1977). *Errors and expectations: A guide for the teacher of basic writing.* New York: Oxford University Press.

Shen, F. (1989). The classroom and the wider culture: Identity as a key to learning English composition. *College Composition and Communication,* 40, 459–466.

Skehan, P. (1989). *Individual differences in second-language learning.* London: Edward Arnold.

Söter, A. O. (1988). The second language learner and cultural transfer in narration. In A. C. Purves (ed.), *Writing across languages and cultures: Issues in contrastive rhetoric.* Beverly Hills, CA: Sage Publications.

Stern, S. L. (1985). Teaching literature in ESL/EFL: An integrated approach. Unpublished doctoral dissertation. University of California, Los Angeles.

Sutman, F. X., Allen, V. F. and Shoemaker, F. (1986). *Learning English through science: A guide to collaboration for science teachers. English teachers, and teachers of English as a second language.* Washington, DC: National Science Teachers Association.

Taylor, P., (ed.) (1989). *From literacy to literature: Reading and writing for the language-minority student.* Los Angeles, CA: University of California, Los Angeles, Center for Academic Interinstitutional Programs.

Trueba, H. T. (1987). *Success or failure? Learning and the language minority student.* New York: Newbury House.

Trueba, H. T. (1989). *Raising silent voices: Educating the linguistic minorities for the 21st century.* New York: Newbury House.

Wolf, D. (1989). Portfolio assessment: Sampling student work. *Educational Leadership,* 46 (7), 35–39.

Wong, J. S. (1945). *Fifth Chinese daughter.* New York: Harper and Brothers.